Vivian Fusillo

Stories Along the
Yellow Brick Road

Contents

Part Four: Vignettes

Part Six: Teaching and Life 274

Part Seven: Health 310

Quotes from Students Who Were Inspired by Vivian 326

Awards Vivian Received 353

Plays Directed by Vivian Fusillo 354
(Winona State University)

Acknowledgments

Special thanks to all who contributed to the making of this book:

Shirley Drury
Madison Ferguson
Bruce Danielson
Bill Kuhl
Sontha Reine Fusillo
Siobhan Bremer
Peter Bremer
Craig Johnson
George Bolon

and all her students for contributing cards and letters.

Foreword

BY SONTHA REINE

Born in a tiny town in Kansas, population 100, during the dust bowl and depression, Vivian found magic in everything from an early age. In her stories of Bogue she recalls the delight of waiting for the mail to be announced by Mrs. Thompson, getting to pick out lumps of coal at the hardware store and spying on her Dad while he barbered and joked with customers, hiding behind the pot belly stove. She played accordion and sang for events at the city hall, as well as yodeling for the annual fair attending at nearby historical Nicodemus.

She would play pretend with her pals in the attic - getting Judy Garland, while secretly wishing she could play Shirley Temple - 'too tall.' Later, as she writes in the Celebrity chapter, she went on to see Judy in concert and meet her in person.

Her mother Rosamond was not quite a stage mom but she set up her daughter's life for success, gently guiding and supporting her to 'get out of Bogue and not spend the rest of your life on a tractor.' Rosamond had a quiet, elegant class and wherewithal that lit Vivian's way.

A favorite story is the one she tells of the farmhands on their homesteaded property, being read Shakespeare and the Bible in the evening, then going off with lanterns to their bunks. Rosamond also played the organ, gave piano lessons, and organized several choral groups including barbershop quartets and bluegrass jam sessions on the porch. Such romantic and charming times are captured through Vivian's detailed and gem-filled memories nestled in this book.

She went on to Marymount College where she started the theater and starred in most of the plays. Later she taught 4th grade at a 'strawberry school' where she met an exceptional student who was in hiding with her mother from NYC. Years later this student, Barb Husted Cook, became a playwright and nominated her for the Kennedy Award, one of many prestigious awards and recognitions she has received throughout her life, including the Main Stage Theater at Winona State University where she directed over 100 plays of every genre, being named in her honor.

Her life reads like a 'six degrees of separation,' all threads somehow leading back around full circle. I gave her a book I found at a Little Library about the actress Pam Grier, thinking maybe she wouldn't be that interested. Upon returning it, she casually told the story of being at one of the performances described in the book (while in San Francisco) where Grier had injured herself and went on stage bleeding. She was sitting next to the director who was going crazy wondering what had happened.

She is always one step ahead, creating, designing, connecting, imagining, inspiring. Vivian's defining quality is Connection - to ideas, art, artists, friends the world over, and former students for which she needs a spreadsheet to maintain lists for her legendary Christmas cards. At the end of the book are a sampling of quotes in praise and gratitude for Vivian's gift of connecting, inspiring, allowing.

Her followers, fans, and friends are countless as evidenced by constant cards and letters, many from former students. Passionate testimonies are in abundance to the life-long influence of her creative, one-of-a-kind style of teaching, directing, nurturing, and challenging that has encouraged so many to success in their own careers and creative lives.

"By taking her cue from us, with her trademark joy and pizazz, she gave us the confidence to go with our own interests and strengths, wherever they might take us, all the way," former student Barb Hustedt Cook wrote, "in my case, from random words and sentences to a story of continuing growth that isn't done yet. And if that's not what it is to inspire, I don't know what is."

She has traveled the world absorbing the people and cultures globally with her trademark passion and joie de vivre and has managed to pen highlights of many of those trips including attending Queen Elizabeth's coronation when the same age as she at the time - 25. And of course, a photograph of her huddling in the rain under tarps appeared in Life Magazine.

In the process she has crossed paths with many celebrities of a staggering range, from living next door to John Gielgud while at Stratford-upon- Avon, hanging out with Mae West and Shelly Winters in California to acting in a Super Bowl commercial with Winona Ryder.

Raising three daughters as a single mom, she designed and

sewed what has become her signature fashion style, as well as clothing for the 'girls.' In between teaching and directing she cooked a sit down dinner every night then often brought the kids along to play small parts in her children's plays. With George, she and the girls traveled to 49 states in a VW camper over their summer vacations. As her family has grown and extended, so has her love and encouragement for them.

And through travels and teaching and raising her family, she managed to set aside time to write, sometimes on the back of envelopes or coffee shop napkins, in delightfully vivid detail about her experiences, capturing a life filled with fun, humor, and love for the world as seen through her eyes. These pages are glimpses of her brilliant life - a gift to connect us all with the magic that is Vivian.

Part One

BOGUE

1

$\mathcal{B}$ogue $\mathcal{S}$tories

A train ran through Bogue, Kansas once a day. It was a great part of my life. We'd hear the train whistle then Mr. Trombley, who was nearly blind, would roll the big wheelbarrow with Mrs. Trombley (Addie, she was called) by his side, holding one of the handles. They'd roll down the 2-1/2 blocks of Main Street to pick up the bags of mail off the train, then roll it to the back door. It was always a mystery to me, and to this day I can hear the squeak of that wheelbarrow.

The post office was next door to our house on Main Street, and my mother would always want me to change my clothes to go. I could never understand that formality. The walls were lined with people who rented mailboxes. I loved to look at the wall of mailboxes with the trim of brass and the tiny little glass doors with the tiny combination locks.

Each one would stand by their box and say NOTHING, just look down. Then Mrs. Thompson, who had beautiful hands, would lift the wooden shutter, look out, and in a beautiful voice would always say, "The mail is sorted." Then everyone got excited and would talk to each other, wondering what they had in their mailbox. It was exciting to dial the number 316, open the little door, and pull out the mail.

I always waited until everyone was gone, and they'd unroll the newspaper and give me the larger sheets of white paper to use for artwork. This was a Big Event every day at 11am in my early life.

We could only afford to heat the barbershop and the kitchen on cold days or laundry days. The barbershop had a beautiful, big round stove with a cracked patterned window in the front door, which made it seem warmer than it was seeing a red glow through it.

I loved our kitchen stove. On one side was a boiler for water to heat for the laundry, which was mostly small barber towels my father used for shaving customers. On the other side, lumps of coal were placed and they caught on fire somehow. They heated the water and the oven. This was the only time my mother baked and she'd make a most extravagant apple pie topped with real farm butter, or spicy muffins.

My part of the 'ceremony' was I got to take the coal bucket (I loved that shape) about a half block to the hardware store and go in a little room all by myself and choose each lump of coal to fill the bucket. I had no idea of time as I carefully picked out each lump.

Oh, I must make a correction. We had a stove in the living room which we heated only at Christmas or when all the Bogue Democrats gathered to listen to President Roosevelt's Fireside Chats because we had the best reception in town.

Growing up in Bogue didn't involve much travel. On Sunday we often drove to the farm. I went to church with Aunt Sarah, my Everything Aunt, even sometimes minister. My mother stayed at the farm and washed the kitchen floor. It never dawned on me that it was her home growing up.

Maybe a few times a year I went with my folks to Hill City (the county seat) and parked at the courthouse, and I got to go into a meeting with the lawyer and decide what crop was to be planted next year. I remember after all the talk of the men, Uncle Ray, Cliff and Dad, my mother said, "Wheat," and that's what was to be.

Once a year we had the Big Trip to Salina and nearby Gypsum for my dad's family reunion. All my aunts and uncles and their kids danced, sang, and played instruments. My mother sat quietly on the side. On the way home, Dad would park in front of Woolworth's so I could look at all the shiny jewelry.

Once a year, the excitement was almost too much when the big pink, yellow, etc. cars came through town filled with Black folks all dressed up with Big Hats, laughing – some from California. They were on their way to the Nicodemus Fair – celebrating the freedom of the slaves.

This was SO exciting!! Among lots of history, if the slaves made it to Nicodemus, they were freed – the Underground Railroad. No Whites were allowed overnight but I was told stories of my folks being the only Whites that had a stand at the fair. I was a fat baby (two-year-old) that could yodel. I was left with the Switzer's stand to yodel for the customers.

A few years later they still had a stand but I was allowed to roam among the stands, and I still remember standing (in the dark) by the concrete dance floor trimmed in colored lights, listening to the wonderful music and watching the dancers.

Memory Moments

30 cents

I found 30 cents on a shelf in the kitchen. I was going to take it so I could join the Girl Scouts, but I knew 30 cents would buy a meal for our family – 10 cents for hamburger, 10 cents for a can of vegetables and 10 cents for a loaf of bread, so I put the money back.

If

My father could and did fix everything. I was standing, watching him work on our car. He said, "If you were a boy, I'd teach you how." I'll never forget his eyes as he looked up from inside the engine and smiled up at me.

Shampoo

Sitting in the barber chair and having lots of shampoo put all over my head, then my dad would create different shapes and extreme designs for me with the shampoo. It was a special time and I would lose the outside world.

Icehouse

Going down to the river and watching my dad cut big chunks of ice and put them in our icehouse surrounded by straw to make them last longer. We had the only icehouse in Bogue. He'd sell the ice to those who had ice boxes. The kids in town spent hours playing 'Andy Over.' Someone on one side of the house would throw the ball over, and if it was caught, that person would run around and tag a person on the other side. Lots of screaming and laughing. I forgot those icehouse days until on a trip to China I looked down at all the soldiers found below ground level.

Bread

Once a week Mrs. Belleau would bake a wonderful bread. She lived on the edge of town, three blocks away. I was given a dime and worked my way past three blocks of houses that I never ever saw, except while on that one errand, including the one we all thought "evil" things went on in there, to buy ONE LOAF of that Wonderful Warm Bread. On the subject of bread – my favorite for a special afternoon snack was dried Holsum white bread with mustard.

Greek Bread

Students in the Theatre Department loved to be with the girls and were the best babysitters. They played games, dress up – all different things I didn't have time to do. One weekend I took a wonderful train ride to Chicago to be with friends. To share the weekend with the girls, I bought a HUGE ROUND BREAD from a Greek bakery to take back to them. On the train ride home, I got restless and tired of looking at all the people, so I dug a little hole in the side of the big round bread and snuck one little bite. As the hours of the ride went by, and the regular click of the wheels, well, I stole more and more little bites from the inside. When the train stopped, I had eaten the entire inside leaving only the huge sunken outside crust of the formerly Big Round Greek Bread to show them!

Girl's Bike

I was the first in Bogue to get a Girl's Bike. Daddy had put it together and painted it RED. He took it out in front of the barbershop and all my girlfriends lined up to learn to ride it. I was last in line. I think my folks "didn't want to spoil me." We were the only family in Bogue with one child.

Kid's Haircut

My dad had a rule in his barbershop. When he cut a child's hair – if the parent stayed to watch and direct, he charged double.

Kitchen Floor

Our tiny kitchen had an old-fashioned black stove with a reservoir for water on one side, a place for the coals, an oven, and a shelf above called a warming oven. Another side of the room had a cabinet with shelves below covered with a narrow marble slab counter which was left over from a grave marker my dad was going to make for my brother who died years before I was born. I once overheard them say the baby fit in a shoebox, was born without kidneys, and my mother refused to look at him because she wouldn't be able to let him go.

On the opposite side wall hung a small mirror – the only one in the house except the huge ones in the barbershop. Underneath the mirror was a small cabinet that held a bucket of water with a dipper and a pan where we washed. I first experimented with make-up in this mirror. The fourth side was a little alcove with windows. There was a small table and three chairs. The floor was covered with a green and yellow little zig-zag shaped pattern linoleum. It became well-worn and the pattern almost disappeared in front of the stove where we stood to keep warm.

One day I found my mother on her knees with a tiny brush, filling in the worn spots with paint. She asked me if I wanted to help and got one of her brushes from her oil painting box. It was a special time with Momie.

Pogue Memories

Shari called and wanted to know if I "needed" transportation through the sleet to the Acoustic Cafe and I DID. I found "my booth" empty and continued the book to the chapters on the culinary world of gourmet cooking. I have NO MEMORIES TO RECALL ON THIS LEVEL. Santha recalled all my "creative cooking" dishes but – I am blank.

In my world (during the depression) for a meal for three was, "change your clothes," go to the store for bread (10 cents), and a can of veggies (10 cents). Only on laundry days when water needed to be heated in the kitchen stove – to wash the barber towels – my mother baked the richest apple crisp pie (with chunks of REAL butter), because she believed if you're going to do something DO IT RIGHT, and very spicy muffins.

My two early art lessons consisted of getting to put the little package of orange coloring in the white margarine and swirling it until it was smooth. The other was going to the only grocery store in our town of 100. (On Saturdays, farmers came to town with produce and watched corn husking contests. My Uncle Cliff always won.) When they got in a huge vat of peanut butter, I got to stir the oil on top until it was smooth and no longer made patterns. We couldn't afford to buy it.

When we went to the farm, I always let my cousin Alson know I was from the "city." He got even. He told me the plants growing by the barn were growing washcloths. I checked daily to see what color. Years later when I had children, I told them this story so when friends took us all to visit the vacant, falling down house and barn, my oldest daughter, without putting on the boots I had purchased to walk through the snake ridden ground, jumped out of the van and ran to the barn to check on the washcloths. She was so disappointed. I told her they weren't "up yet."

Cousin Al took me (age?) out to see the wind in the corn fields. I loved it and went running through the field. Meanwhile, he went back home and left me there alone... it got dark. I made my way through all the shapes and scary things, hoping to find my way back. I made up lots of scary stories in the house later.

Rabbits were eating the crops, so on Sunday afternoon my dad got ready to go to the farm and help. I begged to go along even if I sat in the car. All the farmers met with huge sticks like baseball bats and so many of them each took a side of the field. They walked from all sides and drove the rabbits to the center and killed them with the bats. I cried all the way home.

Work/Play

I've never thought I ever 'worked.' It was always fun. Our house was always clean, but I don't remember my mother ever talking about cleaning. We made everything a party.

There were always 'barber' towels. She washed them and Dad created a ringer that I got to operate. Then I loved hanging them all out on the long clothesline and making designs with clothes pins. I still love that shape - even had Siobhan take a photo of Andy Warhol's HUGE one in the Chicago gallery many years later.

I got to 'help' Anita Kenyon in her drug store across the street. Her sister always wore a full apron over her dresses which annoyed Anita because of the extra work. I got to iron the aprons and sometimes even got to dip the ice cream for a customer. I spent time watching the blacksmith 'shoe' horses - also across the street. I also spent time at the Print Shop. It was listed as the print shop in the smallest town in the US. They printed posters and flyers for sales and barn dances, etc. and they gave me all the 'cut off' paper for art.

If we weren't playing 'dress up' in our attic, I spent hours watching and helping Mrs. Trombley at the cafe. Smoky Barbie would come in with the other men in their boots and big cowboy hats and order a quart of beer each. Mr. Trombley (Fritz) would slide one down the counter to each cowboy. I was allowed to watch - from the kitchen. When I had a customer, which wasn't often, I got to 'take their order' and Addie would have me run out the back door across to the grocery store to buy two pork chops, or whatever they ordered and say to Fritz, "Stir the gravy," while she got the potatoes ready.

A couple drove through town and stopped to eat. He wore a suit and she had on a navy-blue suit and NAVY pumps. I was SO EXCITED. She asked where the bathroom was. I didn't know if we had one and told her, so she asked for a toilet. SO, wearing her 'pumps,' I led her out the front door, across the cracked slabs of cement to our outhouse. I was so worried about her ruining her pumps. They left me some money on the table. I ran across the street to show my mom. I thought they forgot it and ran out to the car to give them their money. They said it was MINE for good services.

My mother somehow got ahold of a rubber scraper no one had seen. She put some oil in a jar, and I went door to door demonstrating how it was used, and sold them for a few cents to almost every house.

A group came to town and needed someone from Bogue to go with them to sell Bibles. I got to go! They collected lots of money but No One Got a Bible!!

We had 'something' my dad created that if you pumped the

stick back and forth it supposedly cleaned our only rug - a worn Persian rug. I got to do that.

I loved to go in the bank and see all the farmers. I asked if I could water their trees. So, I pumped buckets of water from our windmill (the only one in town), carried it across the street, and put two buckets of water on each of their four trees.

Halloween

When we lived in Nacogdoches, Texas – for Halloween the kids shouted, "trick or treat" and they came in and "performed a trick." The black kids insisted on coming to the back kitchen door. They would do their "trick" in the kitchen. It was a real show with singing and dancing!

When we moved to Winona, Santha designed very clever ghost costumes for the three of them. She wrote a script and they rehearsed it. In those days it was safe to go alone. They did. They were so upset no home would let them perform – all but one, a nun. Most homes just handed out the candy. They came home SO disappointed.

Trip to Nicodemus

When I was a baby, I was often left at the Switzer's stand to be watched – as a sort of showpiece I guess, and by the time I was two, I was big into yodeling.

I spent hours watching the local Blacks in their wonderful clothes, dancing wildly to live jazz musicians – waiting on a platform surrounded by little colored lights. Some would sneak off to the back of their car for a drink. I assume alcohol was illegal in Kansas. It was probably homemade. I would sneak in the dark and hear them laughing. It was so exciting to a little kid – peeking.

On Sunday my dad and I would drive to Nicodemus and park outside the church which would ROCK with their voices. My dad would sing along with them but be sure to leave before they came out after the service.

My father, Hubert Akers, was a barber in Bogue. The black men would come by and tap on the front window and say, "How 'bout a shave, Hubert?" then laugh and laugh and wave at him. I never got the joke.

Nicodemus didn't have a high school, so they came to Bogue. They were all my special friends, so I got voted into everything including the basketball team. Of course, we won and were known nationally for athletics. I never understood why none of the black athletes came to the yearly banquet until years later when my girls were 8 & 10.

They all wanted to visit my hometown of Bogue, Kansas. I finally gave in. We borrowed a van from a friend, Dr. Shaffer, and drove to Bogue. I had told the girls so many stories, I was afraid we'd find my childhood home as just a withered pile of wood on Main Street. Bogue wasn't even on the map.

We had many adventures on the way, including stopping at a post office in a town called "Vivian." Santha was in charge of the map.

We arrived, and when they saw a little sign in cardboard that said Bogue, we got out and danced around it. We parked in front of "our" barbershop. Word spread fast that we were there. We slept in the van that night.

In the morning there was a pickup truck parked in front of the now closed drug store. That was where I and two other girls had sung – well sort of harmonized "You Are My Sunshine." My mother sat in the dark on the porch swing directly across the street and listened and waited for me to come home and tell stories. My mother said if I had a piece of candy I'd run over and share it with her.

Back to the pickup truck and the woman in it. Santha ran over to look in the windows of the drug store. The black woman in the truck said, "Come here girl. Are you Vivian Aker's girls? I heard she was in town." Santha then ran to the garage where three men were whittling. She asked about Calvin (he'll be described later) and they said, "It's a good thing your mother didn't marry him. He went to jail."

You see, in high school, Calvin Baumgardner was my boyfriend - I pretended. He was so cute. He had curly hair and such a low forehead I thought his hair might grow down to his eyebrows someday. Well, one day Alvina Balleau took him away (she was really evil). I had the type of skin that if you marked it, it raised and stayed raised for a long time. I actually had heard of someone at the World's Fair with similar skin, and with his shirt off, people would come by and write on him. Well, Alvina made a big 'C' on my arm with her pencil and the skin raised up. I was also wearing a blue taffeta dress with little pink dots glued all over it. I have no idea where my mother got it. Evil Alvina used her nails, and with a long swipe down, removed the dots.

I found out the woman in the truck was Mrs. Switzer from 'the stand,' and mother of several of the star athletes. We invited her to come with us to the only restaurant for a drink. After much persuasion she said, "Well, maybe just a 'sody pop'," but she insisted on going in the back door. She looked like Aunt Jemima with her head in a kerchief and her big chest. She held both twins in her arms and when it was time to move on, they wanted to stay with her and not leave.

We went into Nicodemus. It just happened to be the big Fair Celebration. It had really diminished, but there was a man tinkling on an old piano with a few little colored lights around the piano and a trio of women singing. Their voices rang across the wide-open prairie. Santha cried at the beauty of it all.

Siobhan & I made another trip back many years later. We

drove to Nicodemus. They were doin' up the old church. We found Mrs. Switzer, age 101 and nearly blind. She said, "Vivian Akers, uh uh uh."

A long article in the New York Times was written about the history of Nicodemus including the Switzers. The Switzers are now gone, but not the wonderful memories.

$\mathcal{A}$ is for $\mathcal{A}$nimals in $\mathcal{M}$y $\mathcal{L}$ife

I never had a pet in Bogue, nor did any of my friends. There must have been dogs at the farm, but I only have memories of chickens, cows, and pigs. I remember we got a goat, not for a pet, but I guess for goat's milk to help my dad's stomach problems. But that didn't work out. The clothesline fell down and the baby goat got loose and chewed up all the barber's towels I had hung up for my dad's barbershop.

We had chickens once, but my dad gave them all a name and we couldn't kill or eat them, so I guess they were sold. I do remember a crate of tiny baby chicks arrived and one was dying. The crate was in the back yard and my mother was SO sad because it was dying and suffering. She couldn't do it, but she asked me to drop a rock on it to stop its suffering. It was Very Hard, and we both stood there. I don't remember if I dropped it.

We had a sow – I guess that's what it's called – who had given birth to little piglets. It was a really cold night and my dad brought them into the warm barbershop. Mom tore up a blanket and wrapped each one in a piece of it and then handed me one and a little bottle and I got to help feed them.

Years later in Winona, the family had a bird and when it got very ill George came and took it away for us.

Also, the kids had a pet turtle. We were going on our summer trip and George called the city about what minerals they were putting in the lake. It was safe. So, we went down to the lake and Santha said goodbye to it and put it in the sand, and it found its way into the water.

Outhouse Monsters

On Saturday afternoons, it was a special treat to get to go to the farm where my Aunt Sarah, Uncle Ray and Al, Earl, and Uncle Cliff lived. I had so many adventures, but we'll concentrate on one.

They had an outhouse, so I ventured out to it – maybe equal to a block from the farmhouse – *Alone*. It had three holes, which was a mystery to me, and the other two were very scary.

To back up my story – I opened the wood door with squeaky hinges and stepped inside. My mother would say, "I mustered up my courage." For some reason I thought I had to lock the door even though there was no one around for miles. The hinged door hung crooked, so it was very difficult to reach up and make the lock work.

I sat down – I dare not look at the other two holes for fear of seeing ugly monsters. A Sears Roebuck catalog was the toilet paper. I opened up the catalog and hundreds of moths flew all over. I was so scared I was shaking and had a hard time unlocking the rusty door. When it finally gave in, I ran and ran as fast as I could to the house, thinking the moth monsters were chasing after me the whole way back.

City Hall

Every two weeks, a traveling theatre company came to Bogue. The whole town attended. They had the same people playing different characters with a somewhat different script. There were jars of beans across the front of the stage and we were given a piece of paper to guess how many beans were in the jars. My mom and dad attended and it was the only time I can remember they were ever in public together in Bogue. During intermission, they would come up and the audience seemed so tense. I heard my mother say, "If my name is called, I won't go up."

The City Hall was built in 1937. This changed my life. The Toby Players, and an even bigger deal, was once a week. The hall turned into a roller skating rink with wonderful music. The owner was a very handsome older boy. For some reason he chose me to skate with. I seemed to be able to sway around corners with him even when we were dangerously close to the wall. He was a real show off because he always pretended to have to fix his shoestrings and skate on one foot.

He asked me and another couple to go on a date to a nearby fair. All I remember is we ran out of gas on the way home and by the time he walked me to the door it was past midnight. He said good night and started to leave, and I started into the house, then he turned and told me I was a wonderful skater and KISSED ME and quickly left.

I thought my father was on the other side of the door listening and I was furious. When I told my mother that she said, "I'm not going to stay up that late to hear a kiss." I think I was disappointed she didn't care or pretended not to.

My Dad's Homemade Cigarettes

I found a little bag with a string to tie it closed, and it brought back wonderful memories. Sometimes – between customers at the barbershop – my dad would go outside. He'd pull a little bag that contained tobacco out of his pocket, then take a thin paper out of a folded packet and put the rest back in his pocket, and the rest was magic for me to watch.

He'd hold the one thin piece of paper in his left hand – like a trough – and fill it carefully with tobacco. Then he'd lift the bag of tobacco carefully to his lips and pull the strings to close it and put it back in his pocket – all this while holding the filled paper steady in his left hand. Then he'd take the filled paper slip with both hands and lick it carefully, then seal it. Then he'd twist one end to close it and put the cigarette in his mouth, ready for a big match he'd strike on his pants, and light it.

Not one drop of tobacco was lost. He probably didn't know I was watching – anyway didn't let me know. It was better than TV that hadn't been invented yet.

My Dad

I was so close to my mother and worshiped my dad. He was so charming with a real sparkle about him – a wonderful storyteller. When I was little, I'd sneak into the barbershop (a front room in our house) and hide behind the big pot bellied stove to listen to him until I was caught and sent away.

My girlfriend and I would go into the shop through the front door and ask for a penny. He made a big thing out of giving us both a penny and we ran to the store (two doors away) to buy cherry candy and put it in a glass of water for a very special drink. He also let me sit in the big barber chair and shampoo my hair. He'd put in lots of foam and reshape my hair into all sorts of things. I'd watch him stand like a dancer and with his razor strap sharpen his razor to give a shave. He could and did fix and repair anything.

He would fix cars and bikes when there were no customers. Once I was watching him work on a car and he looked up and smiled and said, "If you were a boy, I'd teach you how to do this."

Although we were very poor, my mother insisted the living room walls should be covered with a sort of warm beige embossed wallpaper. Dad would take a long strip, cover it with paste in one long swoop, then fold it carefully, stand on a platform he made and with one beautiful movement, it would go across the ceiling perfectly.

My mother had terrible hay fever. Before I was born, they'd drive to Colorado Springs, and by the time they got there it was over. He'd barber on the way and find work there while she'd sit in the car on a busy street where she could write.

I have no memory of how he got sick. He was always very thin. My mother decided she didn't want me 'to end up' in Bogue on a tractor, so we three went to Salina. A Big, Big City for me. It was during the war, and we couldn't find any place to stay. I remember us all in the same bed in a basement while looking everywhere to live. I was a senior in a big high school. I don't remember anything except the boys wore jeans and white shirts and the girls wore pleated (all the way around on a waistband) skirts. I never joined the fashion.

I got a job in the Red Hen Cafe and made lots of tips and loved it. My dad worked for *another* barber and HATED it. I started at Marymount College – all girls Catholic (except me) school with rich kids. My dad went back to Bogue but had almost no business. That's when he may have started his stomach problems that turned into cancer. I'm skipping all details of meeting Bob at the USO, playing in the band, and his coming to Bogue to meet everyone at the town hall with his folk singing.

I remember his being in the hospital in Salina and getting upset and walking out in his hospital robe. Somehow my mother arranged for him to move to Gypsum and stay at Aunt Leona's (his sister's) house.

He became very ill with cancer. I was in college and dating Bob, working at the Red Hen and in plays. In the end my mother couldn't trust any of his sisters to watch over him, so she was with him every hour and exhausted, so I'd take the train from Salina (at school) to Gypsum and sit up with him during the night and take the train back the next morning for classes.

Bob (in the Air Force) would read my lessons and try to put the info into my head enough for me to pass. Skipping details, I was sitting with him (heavy on morphine) when he died.

Sometimes Bob would take the train down to be with me. That night he didn't, and I remember going out in the dark and walking tracks hoping he'd come.

At Marymount the nuns decided I had talent, so they created a theatre major for me. I was to give a full evening recital performance for graduation and my dad died the day before. The newspaper headline said, "In spite of father's death, Vivian Akers will perform."

I have no memory of the funeral.

His Obituary:

Huber Elwood Aker, son of Cornelia Ann and William Jaco Akers, was born June 25, 1886, in Ray Co. Missouri and died in Gypsum, Kansas on May 21, 1947.

The first 17 years of his life were spent in Ray Co. In 1903, the family moved to Laredo, Kansas, there to Gypsum where he grew to manhood.

He was married to Rosamond Bondy of Bogue, Kansas on June 29, 1917. To this union two children were born, a son

Forrest Elwood who died in infancy and a daughter, Vivian Rosemary of the home.

Most of his life was spent in or near Bogue, Kansas where he will be long remembered for his many acts of kindness and great friendliness. Hubert loved people and collected friends as other people collect flowers. He was a loving husband and father, and his greatest joy was in his family.

Although he has suffered greatly in these last months of his illness, he was ever cheerful and patient in the care of his loving wife and daughter and other near relatives. He united with the Methodist church and his last month on earth was spent in constant prayer and testimony for his master.

Playing Judy Garland

I just watched a documentary on Judy Garland's life which brought back connections long forgotten.

When I was "little," I don't remember how old, a few girlfriends and I climbed up a ladder fastened to the wall of the barbershop. It was a real trick to climb the ladder and push up the big heavy LID to the attic. You held on to the ladder with one hand and REALLY pushed to lift the big lid so it would fall open, and with a giant step raise yourself into the attic by holding on to the rafters. We did it many afternoons. It was a place not ever inhabited by parents. We played "movie stars." There was a huge trunk of "stuff" we dressed up in, and looked over some old movie star magazines. No idea where they came from.

I always wanted to be Shirley Temple, but I was too tall and had straight hair, so I had to be Judy Garland.

When it was time to come down, my mother would tap on the lid several times with a broom handle. We'd take turns carefully maneuvering ourselves one at a time to Reality.

In the attic was the only time I smoked. We rolled my dad's cigarette papers around some stolen coffee grounds and nearly set the house on fire.

A few years later a theater group traveled the Midwest called the Toby Players. I think they came once a week with a different play and the same characters. The whole town went including my mother, who later never went outside around Bogue except to the back yard and of course to the outdoor outhouse.

Well, one big deal was jars of beans that were placed in the front of the stage by the footlights. When we entered the hall, we were given a paper to guess how many beans were in each jar. At inter-mission they pulled out the winning slips. All I really remember is sitting next to my mother and her saying, "I'm not going up, I'm not." Why did she even enter the guessing game?

The second unknown is how I got chosen, asked, or PUSHED into being an intermission act singing Judy Garland's "It Never Rains but What It Pours," playing Wine, Women, and Song on the accordion, and doing a chalk drawing to music once. I do remember an evil girlfriend said, "I saw the pencil drawing. She didn't make *that* up." It wasn't called bullying then.

Fashion from Pogue to College

I don't remember my mother sewing my clothes – I just remember she once said, "I hate every stitch I take." I have drawings of dresses she designed when I was a baby.

I do remember she did a major part of a dress then turned it over to Aunt Sarah for all the details – buttons, snaps, hems. Once she forgot to sew (just basted) one sleeve in a white organdy dress with different size dots. I loved that dress. However, when I first wore it to school – so proud – someone (maybe the 'evil' Alvina Balleau) grabbed my shoulder, and the SLEEVE CAME OFF!

Another memory was she had made me (created) a skirt out of beautiful blue soft wool, but it had tiny moth holes in it. She gave it to Aunt Sarah who embroidered little flowers around each hole. I loved it.

She must have sent for a 'thrift box' because I had a dress to go on a trip to Oklahoma City to visit Aunt Sarah's sisters. It was cotton – black with Mexican designs and rows of elastic at the waist. Maybe it came from Sears/Roebuck. I know my shoes did. I had LARGE feet and it was hard to find shoes that fit.

In All-Girls college, all Catholic but me, we had to sit properly with ankles crossed. I sometimes had to go to class with jeans and a man's white shirt because I didn't have time to change from building sets and doing lights. Sometimes even a beard if I had to play a man's part in a scene! Every event was Strictly Formal.

I was with a group of girls at Marymount – called the 'Terrible Ten' – during any free time between classes 'cause otherwise I waited tables and got Big Tips. For my birthday, they gave me a Ship & Shore blouse – I hated it. They all wore tiny pleated-all-around skirts.

I was in a play and wore a very beautiful suit from Saks 5th Ave. My mother had me buy it.

Part Two

EVENTS AND OCCASIONS

Meeting the Fusillo Family

Where to begin – what do I remember – years later? I went to New York to meet Bob's parents before we were married. Bob met me at the airport, and we took a train to Baldwin where they lived. Just outside their home, he set down my suitcase and said, "Now talk to my mother about flowers." I think the only flower I knew was a sunflower from Kansas. "Dad will be on the radio and want to show all his equipment." I had never heard of Ham Radio. "Talk to Paul about race cars." And we went in the front door.

Their house was beautiful – all Early American furniture. I didn't think of it until years later, the contrast of living in Bogue and my childhood. I loved our house with the broken steps in the front. We were very poor – Depression – and had very little furniture – nothing matched. The only important piece was the piano (refer to another story). I went to the store to buy food and they told me they couldn't charge anymore. I went home crying to my mother and she said, "We can always sell the piano." Back to Bob. On each piece of furniture, Mrs. Fusillo (I didn't dare call her Helen) had placed a framed picture of Joan – Bob's former girlfriend. Paul was curled up on the carpeted floor. Mrs. Fusillo kept her distance and Mr. Fusillo gave me a Warm Smile and said, "Come into my office." All the walls were filled with ham radio equipment. He put on his headphones and said to someone in another country, "I want you to meet a friend of mine – say something, Viv." Ugh.

I learned later Bob had told Paul that I was Indian, and he was very disappointed. He told Bob, "She doesn't even *look* Indian." We later became good friends when he tried on a metal belt I was wearing, and it fit him – small waist!

Somehow, we managed to get to the kitchen and sit in a booth and have dinner with Mrs. Fusillo serving – not joining. A HUGE bowl of salad was put down and a ritual of vinegar and oil (which I had never tasted) was passed. I thought I'd have some later (there was too much emotion going on) so I passed the bowl and Mr. Fusillo took it and with his hand wrapped around this enormous bowl - ate the rest. I have no more memories of day one.

Bob wanted to take me to Jones Beach. I had no swimsuit – couldn't swim and didn't want to go because I thought the beach was named after Joan – Bob's former girlfriend. Mrs. Fusillo said she'd take me shopping for a swimsuit. It was a HUGE store and when we got to the right department, I was amazed. She tore through the choices and decided I was a different size top and bottom and ended up taking one of each from separate suits and threw the rest back. We stopped at her favorite bakery on the way home (I can still see her *carefully* holding the box with her delicate hand on the strings).

Our routine soon became:
1. Go into the city to see a Broadway show or go to hear Count Basie or Mingus
2. Get home very late or early morning
3. Wake Paul up to go with us to the beach

Oh, I forgot – the 2nd day there we went to the Car Races with Paul. Wow! We tried to get Mrs. Fusillo to go with us – she wouldn't.

Other Moments

The three of us were at the grocery store and somehow found out she thought I was going to *live in New York*. While shopping she asked questions. I said I was going to teach high school in Florida. She dropped the bag and said, "Why?"

A little back up. My father had suffered for years with cancer. When he became very ill, my mom moved him to his sister's in

Gypsum – a few miles from Salina where I was going to college. Bob was in the Air Force. My father stayed at Aunt Leona's (my favorite of all the aunts and uncles) until he died. We had no insurance and enormous bills. My mother had not taught for years (first 3 grades) and was forced to go back to college summer school. We got jobs together in Formosa, Kansas. She was the principal and I taught typing, bookkeeping, and shorthand with a BA degree and NO education classes, NO certification. This was Totally Beyond Belief – Bob planned to return to Salina and go to college.

Another Incident

Something went wrong and Mr. Fusillo lost his temper and threw something and yelled at Mrs. Fusillo - Helen. Afterward, he was all charm and visited with me. She went all over the house complaining to the ceiling and Bob and Paul ridiculed her, pretending to play a violin!

I must write about our wedding day. It was even more shocking for the Fusillo's (all 3) than my first visits to meet the family. I was 21 and Bob was 20 and needed his parents' signature. Helen REFUSED until Aunt Ted (who I liked so much) talked her into it. We went through years when she *really* liked Ronnie (my sister in law) because she was in theatre!!

She came to visit us in Winona when Shari and Siobhan graduated. When they walked across the stage, she turned to me and said, "That son of a bitch Bob." She came to Lakeland for Santha's birth. She came to England (after lots of persuasive letters) to see Santha (before she grew up.) She and Bob toured London and Paris. Shari kept in contact – I tried.

Another Event

I was told the rest of the family wanted to meet me. They lived in a many-stories-high building in Brooklyn. We arrived – I have NO memory of who or how many were there. Gramma lived on the street level. I only remember the room was packed with a long table that took up most of the room, a stove with huge pans to cook pasta, and a china closet filled with colored liquor bottles.

There were kids running around and I could see into the bedroom where pasta was 'drying' on the bed. They were all Italian except one – she was Irish, and Mrs. Fusillo told me everyone loved *her*. One of the daughters was HUGE – like 300 pounds. I was told several of Gramma's past husbands were there. I didn't meet anyone.

We all sat down. Each plate had a huge chicken breast or maybe a whole chicken. Down the middle of the table were large jugs of seltzer water. I sat by a thin man who (I think) was a past husband, and he told me he just got out of jail to meet me (??). He's the only one who talked to me, and we had fun. Gramma was in a wheelchair with one leg amputated (I think). The rest is a mystery...

Another Fusillo Story

When Bob and I were teaching at Florida Southern in Lakeland, we found out his grandfather lived in Clearwater. He was Gramma's first husband. He came to the US from Italy to become a lawyer and take care of the Italians. He had remarried a lovely woman we called "Aunt Lena." She was beautiful. He was very dapper. He dressed and acted 'with much style.' Somehow, we were told we should go to Clearwater to meet them, which we did on a Sunday afternoon.

He was dressed Very Elegantly and mostly talked to Bob. He insisted Lena always wear a silk dress. They lived in one of their many tourists' cabins. She always cooked lasagna which she reached for from under the sofa! She gave me beautiful lace (some of it I used for Santha's wedding dress) and some taffeta, which I still haven't made up.

We were going to skip a Sunday, but Bob felt strange about Grampa (he never called him that) from something he said. He had once been a Big-Name Lawyer and Rich. Now – no business. So, we went. Bob was given lots of Italian lawyer advice. He was depressed because none of the cabins were rented. He said he had arranged every detail for Lena. She really wasn't allowed to do anything except be Kind and Beautiful.

We left that Sunday. He went to the garage and killed himself. Lena went out of her mind and went to live with nuns. We heard nothing more.

Bolon Reunion

Let's see - how can I remember the Bolon Family Reunion of 2017? The last one was 10 years previous, held in the same town in Indiana, just outside of Chicago where it all began. George's father came over from Greece at 9 years of age to work with relatives on the railroad. It was an arranged marriage with his mother. Over 100 attended - some could only speak Greek. George's mother was the oldest, so she spoke at the reception, held in a gorgeous Greek cathedral. The dinner was held in the most elegant of Chicago's Greek restaurants. The 100 or so went past a long table beautifully set with all kinds of Greek dishes to choose from. It was all organized by a wonderful woman named Carol.

Ok, the year 2017 - it was organized again by Carol. George put aside airport duties (in honor of his mother) to go. She died at 99. We left Winona about 7 am and took the map my car reported. We went through gorgeous country and 7 hours later checked into a beautiful motel. We took a nap, and many pills, to get through this with my stomach problems. Just George and I and two other family members were invited to Carol's beautiful home. I was introduced to her husband Bob (who was in a wheel-chair and couldn't talk), two daughters (very Greek) and two brothers - Steve, a world renowned heart surgeon, and his brother - a big time Shell investor, both retired and authors of books. Before we got there, George told me I could have the doctor look at me - and added, "He's a veterinarian." (It was a George joke.) So when I met him, I started talking about animals I saw on the farm trip. He was confused.

Neither brother looked Greek. They were the only ones who didn't marry Greeks. Their wives weren't there. It was so much fun to watch and listen to George maneuver the various conversa-tions - medicine, finance, politics, sports, teaching, family, food. Steve and I became instant friends as well as Bob (in a wheel-chair). Carol brought out a huge book she kept of pictures and history of the family, including Chicago Mafia and arranged marriages, all on velvet pages. The athletic daughter told me she'd rather talk about theater. They served Retsina wine and plates of baklava Bob had created. (When George was growing up, he and Dean spread butter between many layers of filo dough for his mother's baklava -100 or more for the church bazaar.) Sometimes we all talked at once. A HUGE TV was on (sound off) because the Cubs were playing, and the doctor is such a fan he has it on his license plate.

It was then time to move to the Main Event - quite a contrast! It was held in a newly opened, very plain Greek restaurant - only 25 people, almost no other customers. Two long tables covered in paper with ugly plastic plates at each place and strange decorations. Also, a *huge* contrast of people - all Greek but me. Our table was the 'sophisticated' one at the end. The waiter flirted with me (the obvious foreigner). The doctor (Steve) tried to include me with theater talk. Food was family-style on huge platters, 5 or so to each table. We took what we wanted and passed the plate on. There were five kinds of appetizers and six main dishes. Sometimes the huge man at the end took the plate and what we didn't eat. And then came six desserts. It was non-stop talking.

Across from me sat this huge woman draped in red who felt herself to be very beautiful. She had her hair, makeup, and nails done perfectly and announced that her food was better. She was the mother of the *huge* man at the end and didn't approve of her huge daughter-in-law (in shorts) holding her *tiny* baby on her *huge* chest. Mother did not approve so took the baby away to care for her RIGHT. They had two beautiful children and the little girl danced like a ballerina over to me and asked if she could touch my ring.

I was amazed how George "handled" each style of people. Doctor Steve kissed me goodbye and said, "Get to Chicago and we'll go to the theater." We took *our* map home and got there in five hours. I have a feeling there won't be another, or if so - George won't go. I compared the Greek reunion to the Fusillo reunion after we were married.

Bob and I were invited to Gramma's (the Fusillo clan) "to meet the family" in New York. All lived on various floors of one building in Brooklyn, New York. To set the scene - small rooms were crowded with people, lots of kids running around. Gramma was in a wheelchair (I think one leg removed), Very Loud and Italian. Her two daughters were *huge*, and Gramma's several ex-husbands were there. The room had a huge table, and a china closet filled with colored liquors made for the occasion. There was a stove with enormous kettles to cook the pasta. Some beds were covered with pasta - drying. All were Italian except an Irish girl (who spoke to me a little) and Mrs. Fusillo looking small and German.

Somehow, we all sat down. There was much conversation of who belonged to which father. I sat at the end with an ex who said he was just out of jail. He and I had a good time. No one else knew I was there. The dinner started with a whole chicken and quarts of seltzer down the middle - quite a contrast for me who grew up in a town of 100 in Kansas with very little conversation. I grew up in the Depression - meals were 30 cents - 10 cents for hamburger, 10 cents for bread and 10 cents for vegetables.

Surprise Birthday Party

I have a friend named Chops and his wife Diane, a family with LOTS of money and LOTS of problems. He's done everything - gourmet cook in Paris and Italy, underwater photographer for National Geographic, sold the land for Disneyland, has pieces of the Berlin Wall. He was a Navy Seal, paid for me to fly Peter Pan, etc. It was his birthday and Diane arranged a surprise party. George and I, WSU photographer and people from the Athletic Department he supports. We all arrived at their home - BIG SURPRISE. I led the song. He cried. After drinks, 13 of us got on a Party Bus with disco music and lights. We arrived at Lovechild Restaurant in Lacrosse. Very elegant! The table was beautiful with white candles and white roses. The chef came out to greet Chops. Amazing menu. I was sitting between George, who was talking to the football coach, and a woman with a terrible voice who had taken my class years ago and insisted on telling me every detail. I couldn't take it any longer and saw a couple at the bar that looked interesting - well he did. I went over and asked, "Who are you? You look interesting." He said, "We thought *you* looked interesting." He was in town for a big concert. The more we talked - she realized she knew my daughter, Santha. I went back to the party and *that* woman.

The couple decided to leave and came to our table and asked to have their picture with me. Ugh, OK. Three from other tables so there were FLASHES from three cameras. The picture turned out great and he posted it on Facebook with nice comments and received many 'Likes'. Lesson: After I saw my new driver's license I almost fainted. Now I know if there are three flashes from three cameras it erases wrinkles - coming on so fast with weight loss.

Party Cost $2,500 - Plus bus, tips, and drinks!

Bruce Hittner's Funeral

Bruce's funeral was very special. In his planning, he brought lots and lots of people together for fellowship, to read, tell stories, and play music. He wanted to start at 7 pm with no ending time.

He really became a saint, a shaman with a spirit that will go on and on. They had huge posters and displays of lots of photos from all ages and lots of situations including the wonderful picture of him standing on broken ice – wind blowing, water in his face, playing his saxophone. The urn with his ashes, his old worn hat, his canoe paddle (broken) were displayed. People told stories of living with him when he was a freshman at WSU. Doctors from Mayo told stories and finished a reading they weren't able to do before one of his many operations. An Indian friend told of being called to do the eagle feather cleansing ritual before death. (Bruce left an eagle feather in his will for me – to have courage.) People from Jacque Cousteau told stories, environmental people from all over told of all the things he did, media people, messages from England and France.

The gist of what I said was a mention of memories – coming home when he was building his house to find a little bag and a note saying, "I had enough money to buy nails and a chocolate for you." Another time all of his hand carved pipes from horns and a note, 'Please take care of these. I've gone walking the moon. P.S. - They don't like baths." I told the audience about his guest performance and talk to the oral interpretation class that will inspire us for years – just a few days ago.

Real communication is in silence. I'm glad I had hours of silence with Bruce both on and off stage. I placed a flower and driftwood to last forever by his urn.

Letter - 1968 Delta Queen

This will have to be ramblings, or I will never make myself write and do it. I really lucked out as best that could be. We live in a town nestled between two sets of high bluffs, lakes, and the Mississippi River. It has a very European feeling; in fact, I may be a visiting professor in Europe and haven't been told yet.

The day began with a boiled egg out of Noddy egg cups with hats (English children's book characters). This is a special treat for the girls. Santha and I put together wooden counter stools from Sears (they rock) while the twins made patterns with dried leaves on the front lawn. Siobhan did a pattern on one side, and Shari did another. The lawn was cleared of all the non-orderly squirrels. Only those bright enough to follow the paths could stay.

For lunch we went to Deer Park, and they looked at us while we pet them. I had read an ad in the newspaper about a pick-your-own grape arbor and we drove 30 miles past turkey farms, a buffalo herd, squash, and apples with car top down and burning sun in this 'beginning to change' wonderland of Fall.

On the way, I saw a sign saying Lock & Dam and it looked like a good lane for us, so we did it. A small crowd was gathered. The Delta Queen was coming. We heard the 'toot' and it came in. They stopped to take on freshly selected local foods (our brown Indian bread, butter, and cheese). We caught candy from the passengers, and we cried when the steam calliope played and Santha said, "Oh Momie, that's the best steam pipes in the world!" and the huge red paddle wheels began to turn and a dark black negro in a blue Italian silk sweatshirt waved goodbye - its last voyage. The last of its kind up from New Orleans - a little of Mark Twain.

We picked apples with baskets strapped to our backs. We attended the Oktoberfest in Lacrosse where Emmet Kelly Jr. did his 'didn't talk' act with the girls and looked at me and let a tear roll down...attended a Polka contest...ate bratwurst and kraut on rye. A friend and I wanted to go to the beer tents and didn't know whether to pretend we were in England and leave the kids outside the pub or be American and put them on rides, so we asked Santha and she arranged to read to the twins in the car while we had a bit of the local cheer and shouted with glasses held high each time they opened another keg.

But back to the Delta Queen story. It included memories of merry-go-round riding with my mother and Bob years ago in Central Park with Craig on a rainy day and at the Santa Monica Beach to the Happy song while the operator held a transistor radio close to his ear so he could hear the 'real' music.

We drove on to the vineyards and the kids all picked. Of course, Siobhan had to go to the bathroom.... Then we dashed home to join a crowd in Winona to watch the Delta Queen go by but not stop. An ex-captain is from here. He had gotten on his best dress uniform and signaled, but they didn't stop. The girls went over to cheer him up. All the passengers shouted and waved at us. We are three small colleges, Catholic boy....Catholic girl...and Small but Growing Winona State. St. Teresa's has a swinging art department, headed by Potvin (international fame) and good drama people who were at Catholic U when I was. By balancing calendars and arranging lots of babysitters, I can attend lots of good things. The Philadelphia Chamber Symphony was sooo good after I got over the shock that this was the first time I had attended a concert without a male. We saw Blood Wedding; Lady's Not for Burning is coming up and we're opening with The Rivals on a Guthrie type stage. I saw an excellent actor I knew in England who is now touring the country doing eight well cut complete plays with marionettes. He works them and does the most believable performance of Oedipus I could imagine.

Winona State has a young handsome new president who has a cello in his office for relaxation and booked a game of tennis with me. NO Pressure. I'm breathing so much crisp fresh air and getting such a healthy outlook and even digging up interesting friends.

1. A chemistry wit named Jerry Witt who gave me an antique beaker, hand turned and blown and carved. The guy had trouble with the 8. I put a beautiful, dried tumbleweed in it. He collects cars - has six now. He also makes beautiful sculptures which I can't have because he calls them formulas?

2. I had an elegant European evening at the apartment of Attila Horvath, ex-Hungarian ambassador who was exiled by the Germans... worked for 15 years for the American Propaganda scene and is now publishing a very Hippie Fresh poetry which I'm going to present soon, and cooks many courses with all the

right wines and wants Vivian Breaks, doesn't go in for coffee breaks.

3. There are many others in the Psychology Department, English is a bit low, some in Music...a real young single, dashing pianist who spends every summer studying in France, and took me away with a Russian romantic long, brown suede coat like I've never seen before...his design. As he says, it has so much going for it, he doesn't need to do anything. I understand.

The Head of the Dept. pats me on the bottom, calls me Doll, is elderly, sharp tongued to everyone but follows it with a side glance around her glasses and says 'Cripes' to me. I know my role and it's easy to play. I'm bringing her up-to-date and she needs me badly. I'll direct a Reader's Theatre show...I have a super idea for 10 readers. I have excellent oral interpreters, these German, Hungarian kids fall right into it with lots of pure folk singing and shining hair, using eight guitarists and movies and a light show with the readers. I'm the new director to begin Children's Theatre. Got an idea for a sure opener for me. I'd like to use a tinker-toy set against black curtains. Simple but perfect. I got the only rental house in town...by phone...by luck. It's old, big, and fun. Never have I worked so hard by myself to hang, build, paint and it now looks like a good taste 'boutique.' The girls live upstairs in our castle.

So far, I've had guests every weekend from Macomb. So warm, all different and all jealous so I keep many secrets. Sunday is bad. Who invented it? God? Or was he resting that day? So, we walk miles into the country and 2 blocks to our 2 lakes and watch sailboats and jumping fish disturbing the reflections of the bluffs or dig in the sand for 'a thing' or go to the opposite side of town and watch sky divers behind boats beat it under the bridge before it turns for a barge.

This is Our Year. What next? Whoops, no such thought. Love, past, present, future is a muddle, complicated but something may happen. Bob arrived in Winona with kids naturally and had the fun of seeing. Reading...analyzing all the good things...I arrived in a new town, new job...unseen. New house...furniture piled to the ceiling in one room. Kids excited beyond all reason to see me...Edith in the car out front...the mousy look gone. Full curly tousled hair (like mine with more order) and large ring, LOOK OUT. I felt that they were grandparents driving away. Dull. There were no tears. Fear yes, all the way.

I met a Welch architect who thinks he loves me...lives in Vancouver, writes and calls weekly and will come to visit soon. It's been so long since I've been really loved...I don't know for sure what I feel. He was great at Carmel, Monterey, San Francisco, but there is another possibility who is mostly what I would imagine would come next in many ways, owns banks in the Midwest, fun, real, easy, loves me and I know it...has driven over 500 miles twice to visit the kids. So good with them. I don't know. I don't know how one ever knows. It's a little like cutting a beautiful piece of material. Right and wrong and all the possibilities of it before it's cut. I feel a worldly 15.

I was fortified. I needed it badly. I must keep up the spirits and let what will happen happen. I don't know where I belong but right here is good. I'm less scared of me than I have been in a loooonnngg time. I even have enough confidence to shut up now.

Write, I need to know you're there.

Letter 1978 — Family, Job, etc

What a Beautiful Day. How I wish you were here to share it with. The pretty white snow is covering everything. Santha just came trudging home in the snow – she's so beautiful in every way – she glows and twinkles, big dimples, sparkling eyes, and voice for everyone. She loves living and gets more out of her daily world than any six people. Tabu perfume was my today's present because we had a special walk together earlier. She's finishing a very smart wool suit for our trip to Minneapolis tomorrow. She stops traffic daily. Shari and Siobhan are getting ready to go cross-country skiing down by our lake. They are tall, long-legged, and Gorgeous in a very sophisticated way. They have faces like a fawn, smooth is the word. They love gymnastics, ballet, and boys of any height. Next year they'll be grown up I'm afraid. Santha is a teenager – a sort of sensitive super star – lots of drama, music – she plays guitar, sings, piano, harp and cello, double A honor roll in grades. They're amazing to live with. I slip once in a while into sadness to think how soon they'll be grown, but I'm learning to take a year at a time and see what happens.

Our winters are very busy. Lots and lots of activities together, concerts. We live in a beautiful town with three small colleges so there's lots of good things available. We're nestled between high bluffs with two lakes on one side and the Mississippi River on the other side. The beach is 3 minutes away with sailing available with friends, and the river with barges, river life, and friends with motorboats 5 minutes away.

I can't get over how lucky I was to find this job in this town and some security. We rent a beautiful old home which we've had fun decorating. Santha has created a complete Gatsby room with old lace wall hangings. The twins are all yellow and white and ruffles and Raggedy Ann (I made them life size dolls 6 years ago and they all sit in that old Victorian bathtub we bought in England). My bedroom is grand with mellow brown velvet drapes on six windows that overlook the back garden. I rise in pure luxury every morning then the girls bring me coffee in bed.

I think this was our best Christmas ever because we made things mostly and had lots of surprises. Santha made the twins gorgeous old-fashioned yellow flannel nightgowns with ribbons and lace. I made her a dark brown, floor length skirt patterned with old lace collars, cuffs, and trimmings. It's so pretty I must make myself one I think if I can collect enough old lace things. Siobhan made everyone a little stuffed doll and put it by our pillows, Shari created some clever games out of burlap and felt. We always have a fire, read, and look at Grandma Moses paintings and hang stockings – Santha said she has yet to have a sugar plum fairy dance in her head. Me either.

We had a good summer. If I'm lucky, I get to teach the first part. I teach Creative Dramatics to some 60 local children, then we take a camping trip. You know for years we always went to New York or Europe. Bob was such a snob he thought there was nothing to visit in the U.S. We have found there's a Big World here! The first summer I had the girls, a friend loaned us a VW camper, and without knowing what I was doing, we had a 3-week tour back to my home in Kansas - I had been away 20 years.

It was a super homecoming. We went on to Denver, Colorado, Yellowstone Park, and the Tetons and then home though Wyoming. We went horseback riding in the mountains. We entertained the countryside. The next summer, George - a pilot who's on the university teaching staff - bought a VW van and we all went on another trip, this time to the coast of Oregon and into Vancouver. The next summer we changed directions and went to New York City – first time for the girls – down the coast to Florida and home by way of New Orleans, jazz, and oysters.

Last summer we took a 5-week trip through the southwest U.S. We stayed in gorgeous red rock National Parks, climbed, visited art galleries, Indian Reservations, theaters, gambled 5 cents in Las Vegas, went to Mexico, and fell in love with San Francisco. This summer we plan to take a trip through New England and Canada and there is nothing left but to go to Europe next summer. We'll have to rob a bank, but somehow – we may see you who knows!

I have an excellent job. I can be as creative as I please. I've done some fun things. I directed the first show this year called TANGO. I'm working on the next called Theatre of the Mind – it's an original show on some topic – impossible to describe, but your heads would whirl if you saw one. Lots of multimedia, voices, readings, dance, mime – so it's next. Each spring I do a children's show to 3000+ children bussed in from all the local schools. My classes are very fun, and I love the work. I'm finally getting over some of my fright about whether I'm capable – I have no choice so I am.

It was a HOMECOMING and we had one week to get ready for Christmas and they've been better each year. So enough of us. Jim and Alma, are you still off to the continent doing all those special things? Sue and I felt bad but liked your letter on your illness which you probably don't remember now. Oh, I want to see you all about the house and garden and visit, but I'd also love to have you here with us. You'd like us. We're a good family.

I know it's not fair to ask, but drop me a line and next time I may never stop writing.

Lots of Love,
  Vivian

I Did July

8 Concerts - Beethoven Festival
3 Shakespeare Plays - Shakespeare Festival

Weekend in Wayzata to see Siobhan in Children's Show
Stayed with Alums - John and Janice Hurd - trying to sell their
home on Lake Minnetonka for a million or so.

My daily routine to help handle retirement:

1. From my four closets of clothes I created through the years,
I select <u>What to Wear Today</u> to the Acoustic Cafe.

2. I sit in 'my booth,' write down memories and wait for
alumni from some of the 46 years at WSU to come by and tell me
what I said, wore, assignments (I'm sure it's not true but they give
me much credit and it breaks up my 'retirement depression').

At one of the concerts: The stage at Saint Mary's has a Huge 3-
sided, padded wall. It's rust/orange and well lit. The quartet had

endlessly intense violin playing. The first violinist weighed about 300 pounds. She wore a lime green 'bag.' I got sick from it all and had to leave. Several asked, "Why?" I told them because of the intensity of the color. One person said, "Oh, what color was it!?"

Oh, to have others' vision.... sometimes... I have tiny growths on my skin - and face. I said it's age - the neat Latin Dr. said, "You're beginning to mature." So I may have them 'fried' off - "if they really bother you," he said. That's it except 5 pounds off my middle which means exercise. I'm so bad at a regular routine.

Meanwhile, I made a list of festivals I might go to this summer:
Sand sculpture - Cranberry - Jazz - Music - Art - Motorcycle - Classic cars - Rhubarb - Storytelling - Polish - Chocolate - Shakespeare - Champagne - Butterfly.

1988 Happenings

The adjustment coming home from my adventure is wonderful. I know I'm home. The people all lean forward to smile, say hello or 'help.' It's SO clean. It's SO quiet. I hear every bird's new song outside my window.

When I arrived, I covered the entire town, talked to all the people I knew or knew me or were my students once, and told bits of stories about the Neverland I had just returned from. I biked six blocks to the lake while Shari ran, looking up at the sailboats, almost tipping over and getting deep whiffs of the rose garden.

We took our salad lunch to the Mississippi – 4 blocks away – and sat on the artistic dike created by a former student of mine and watched a big barge go by, water skiers got out of the way just in time, waved at friendly people on the occasional boat going by for the day.

I made a death trip in my yellow convertible to Northwest Fabrics – the fabric store I stop in daily for my therapy (to imagine what I would design out of some fabric to add to my full basement I'm going to do 'someday.' Northwest is CLOSED! I wanted to be there for the last moments to be with the clerks I've known for 15 years of looking.

A Rush of excitement. Summer School begins at 7:30 tomorrow. We'll be going to a chicken barbecue this afternoon with a crowd of pilots and owners of small private planes – many hand-made. It's in a nearby town where a friend built his own landing strip. On the way home we'll stop and pick raspberries. We have tickets for a Historical Society dance (another style of conversation).

Just heard some friends from Maine are coming though. I'll meet them in Minneapolis – maybe stop over with Santha and see the opening season at the Guthrie and dance at Summerfest and hit some yard sales. And it's just six weeks to think about, make clothes, worry – Get ready for a trip to Spain, Portugal, and Morocco.

Zed and Pelly Visit - July 1993
(Letter to Santha)

The world is a better place because of Zed and Pelly. You have the most wonderful kids in the world and you're doing good things. We were out of it when we got home at 2 am. I wanted to write to say the things I never seem to say when I see you.

I awoke early and had so many nice memories. I found little dinosaur stickers on rocks, on blades of grass, on the new lawn I had put in, the lawn mower, the rain sticks which Zed and Pelly used to bring out the sun, and other secret places. Lake was curled up asleep in a basket of the kids' clothes I had on their bed. She really misses them.

I miss them so much this morning. I waited for their call, but their room was quiet. Hopefully we can do it again later after school is out and George's lawsuits are settled, or you can bring them one way. We had lots of New Activities this trip along with repeats. They are so good together.

The Parade: They liked it - all the clowns, lions, etc. came over to our curb seat to give the All-American Kids a gift. I've heard so many remarks about how wonderful they are. The photographer missed getting them in the paper.

The Fly-In Breakfast: Zed wanted to be on the truck with George. It was bad weather so all we had was the stunt plane. Pelly ATE - 2 pancakes, eggs, 3 sausages, and orange juice. We couldn't believe it.

At the Lake: We watched lots of duckies and a Blue Heron was the main attraction. The toy boat wouldn't move enough in the little puddle, so we went into the HUGE lake puddles and the boat really went.

The Carnival: We all walked and looked, and Zed had a LONG ride in the little planes. While I taught class - Shari came in. She and Siobhan took them with Zed riding his bike several blocks and into Windom Park to play in the Gazebo - someday we'll have Princess Winona and the fountain there. They took turns choosing little stickers and placing them on your poster. We went to the post office and saw the mail trucks, so they'll be waiting for them in Minneapolis. They baked 'high energy' bread with George. We had lots of good food in the kitchen with our new bright colored dishes and tablecloth. We made jello with pineapple, blueberries, and marshmallows (they stole).

Dinner at the Big Table was Great. They had already eaten in the kitchen - George barbecued steaks so they ate again - lots of steak, potatoes, beans, asparagus, and pink lemonade. They finished early so I asked them to sit with us and make conversation. They made up words, sounds, sang and giggled a lot.

Quiet Time - sort of: I got smart and after lunch we all went to our beds and read Dr. Seuss books - first me to them, then they to me - then them at the same time for 45 minutes. A needed break!

Lark Toy Shop at Wabasha was great fun for Zed (Pelly was asleep for 2 hours). He loved the carved carousel animals, the Christmas Room, the wonder of it all. It's So Beautiful! The Carousel will be finished and going in 1½ years and hopefully we can all ride. The owner was a professor at WSU once.

A Nice Story: The head of the Carousel will be a dragon - the driver - a Wizard will look like him. On its side will be two bags of fireflies. They'll be hollow inside. He and his wife have it in their will to be cremated and the ashes put in the bags, so they'll ride the carousel forever.

Lots of Barges are moored on the Mississippi because of the flooding. We watched a Tugboat move a big barge and go under the big bridge.

Hopefully I'll get pictures sorted and reprints - one of my many projects planned. Someday I hope to create a cloth book about Zed and Pelly visiting Winona which we'll read together when they come down.

You looked so soft and pretty when you picked up Pelly and Zed to welcome them back. A lovely picture.

I hope you had a good break.

Love,

Grandma Viv

Winona State Homecoming 2011

What a weekend! I had gotten a simple letter saying I had been chosen to get one of the Distinguished Faculty Awards. Typical of my thinking was 'Great, it will be sent,' - a piece of paper through the mail - BUT NO.

Thursday

We (George was also chosen as a recipient) went to the President's office for elegant hor d'oeuvres and mingled with the Board, President, Alum Head, and all his staff. George and I were each given a girl to "take care of all details of our every need" for the weekend. They Really Did. One of the girls made a ring and bracelet for me, and George was given a pen in the shape of a bone for Boguey (our dog). Photos were taken separately with the President and were shown a large gold, engraved medallion "that we'd be given later."

Thursday Evening - A Wonderful Banquet

The whole family except Pelly and Zed (Santha's kids) had one table. The tables were gorgeous with flowers and candle arrangements. There was great live music and then we were called up one at a time (after they read everything about us in the program plus added things). We were given the medallion and SPOKE.

Let's back up-

During the dinner - for the first time ever - some food 'went down the wrong pipe' as they say. I gasped and lost my breath for too many seconds. The music stopped. The entire place was quiet and looking at me, I'm told. Siobhan jumped up and yelled, "HELP! Someone who knows CPR!" (I can't believe she knew the term - she can't either.) George jumped up and called for the Head of Nursing who sat nearby. George performed the Heimlich maneuver on me. I heard the nurse say, "Is she breathing?" I came to, everything had stopped, the President came over and touched my shoulder. George apologized for grabbing me too high and hurting my rib cage. Siobhan left the building, she was so upset. Shari sat with me and talked me back to reality and when I could stand, walked me to the bathroom past all the silent tables except for some that asked if I was alright.

So...

I started my speech saying that I would do anything to get out of speaking. I was told by many my speech was outstanding and got lots of congratulations. It was a BIG NIGHT.

Friday

Up at 8:30 am to attend an alum breakfast. The room was decorated with photos of past alum faculty.

A Break

A break until a Bigger athletic Hall of Fame banquet. Wonderful food and decorations. We were introduced but No Speech. During that afternoon, I fell back into a depression because I felt like it was the beginning of the end of teaching, plus an artist had taken a picture of me and made a big poster of my face surrounded by fall leaves. I looked terrible - No personality - DEAD.

To cheer up for the Hall of Fame banquet, I overdressed in a beautiful, black silk taffeta dress I had made for a N.Y. fashion show maybe 50 years ago. The president said I looked magnificent. A past WSU student (now on the international circle) came over and raved about my beauty, said she used to watch me across campus, was afraid to speak - I was an Icon. The dress worked.

Saturday - There's More

George and I in his Red Corvette convertible were in the Homecoming Parade. I wore purple velvet with a sequin butterfly top and a Purple Feather Boa. (Later at the jazz concert I was introduced as Lady Boa.) Yes, and a purple ring and purple gloves. Our escort girls had made huge posters with our pictures and huge print

GO VIVIAN

GO GEORGE

and handed them out to the crowd along the parade path. My family: Siobhan and Shari, Scott, Brooke, and Bailey got some and held them up high, holding up the car and the whole parade. A surprise! We had been given two huge bags of purple beads to throw along the route and two bags of candy. It was quite a job to unravel the huge bunch of beads and sling them! It was the second parade I'd ever been in. The first was when I was 9 or 10 years old in Bogue, Kansas - my hometown of 100 (on a Saturday afternoon). I marched and played a little piano accordion for two blocks. The straps hurt so much my mother padded my shoulders with towels.

OH - I just remembered a third time. Winona has a Big Festival with a long parade each year. So one year a friend of mine decided the shut-ins at the nursing home should have a parade - this meant going around a small circle twice for those who could sit outside. Well, I was put on a wagon to wave. The chair was rocking, plus a man was afraid someone would steal them, so at the last minute he put three boxes of pet snakes on the wagon next to me. Uh huh!

Back to the Homecoming Parade. We were encouraged to stay for the rest of the parade. An escort parked the Corvette, and we were ushered to special chairs on the sideline even with beautiful blankets just in case we felt cool. NOT COOL! I had felt so removed from WSU, the theatre students - the dept. I felt very distant from the theatre club. They built their float at the airport each year. George moves the jets etc. out so they can build the float in his hangar. We hadn't heard so I felt that was over. I hadn't heard they had asked (late) for this privilege. George and I went outside the airport after a jazz concert to check. I only knew three of the people. They said they were all being celebrities.

Back to the parade -

Their float came by with huge pictures of George and me. One of the girls - tall, very good looking, was dressed like me and sauntered around with her head up and wearing a large ring. I couldn't believe how wrong I was. Oh, one more detail. Our escort girls were wearing T-shirts with our pictures on the back and taking orders. We're almost back to NORMAL. The house is filled with presents, cards, flowers, and HUGE photos of George and I covered with messages.

Part Three

CELEBRITY ENCOUNTERS

Coronation Story

Coronation seats were too expensive. We had a friend with a television set. It would be easier to sit in a comfortable chair and watch everything. As the time arrived and England became fuller and fuller with decorations and tourists, we got excited. We must at least see a plume go by. 'We' means three of us; Bob, Betty (a Fulbright scholar from Georgia) and me.

Betty and I wore slacks and sweaters, Bob a tweed suit. In as much as the wireless had been announcing for days that the police would take all chairs, luggage, etc. away from the crowd, we had but two blankets. Sunday afternoon about 4 pm the three of us walked out our front door across the street and raised our thumbs. We stood about 10 minutes under a rainy sky, a car stopped, we leaped toward it - a woman asked in a dainty voice the way to Ipswich - Dud! While a big black car came tearing around the corner I jumped up in the air and waved my thumb.

He stopped and made a record trip. London in 1 hour and 50 minutes (bus time is 4 hours).

London was packed with restless people from every corner of the world. Some were looking at decorations, some were going home from work but everyone had the same thing on his mind – the Coronation. Around and around we walked trying to choose the ideal spot to sit and watch the parade. Thousands of others were doing the same. Suddenly we heard cheering and saw people running – we followed. The Royal Family and many American actors were going into a nightclub to see Noel Coward. The closest we could get was almost a block away, and even by jumping up or climbing on shoulders it was impossible to see anything. If we were to see the Queen we must carefully choose our spot and get there early!

We spent the night at the Youth Hostel for 30 cents each. In the morning after breakfast we walked out to buy a newspaper. The headlines said people had begun camping on the Mall (the main road to and from the Palace) since 4 that morning. No time to lose. We headed for the Mall and walked the full length looking for a wide lamp post to lean against but all such luxurious stations were taken. The next best thing was to park on the curb where the sidewalk was the narrowest so the sure-to-be-seething crowd wouldn't be so likely to push us from our place. Down went one blanket on the gravel, the other one to serve (if we needed it) for warmth and protection from rain. We needed it! 10 am Monday.

Twenty-four hours and 30 minutes later the Queen would be leaving the palace.

Within an hour, the space around us was packed with fellow campers and the Mall was already a parade of sight-seers and seat-hunters. Bob held our places while Betty and I went shopping for a two days supply of food. By noon, all along the route, campers were settled for the night. We returned and Bob took a look around and took pictures of the decorations.

Enormous arches crossed the Mall, painted blue. On top stood four huge gilt lions holding up a crown. A crown about 10 feet in diameter hung from the arches. On the blue-painted lamp posts were four gold trumpets holding wine-colored banners on all four sides and at the top a gold crown glittered. We were very close to the Admiralty Arch which was ablaze with gold anchors and ropes. Much of the filming of the procession for the movie took place on top of the arch and by a photographer up in back of where we sat.

We were like a big happy family in our section. One nearby couple brought four children and near us sat a 71 year-old woman who had seen the last Coronation and was determined to see this one. The first of the many rains came. We bought newspapers to put on our heads, but by 4 pm our blanket was soaked. We had to keep our feet up because of the dirty water running down the gutter. The closest specially built 'comfort station' was a block away, but it took an hour to fight through the crowd. All day and all night legs and feet of every description passed us. Chapped white legs of little girls, big boots of hitch-hikers, high heels and nylon hose, black shiny shoes with gray spats; they kept walking all through the night. The temperature dropped to 44 degrees and our blankets were wet but we sang and the idea of a queen in a gold coach kept us cheerful.

HUDDLERS, bundled under blankets and plastic ponchos, stick together on curb in Trafalgar Square.

At 3 am the police force came on duty with the news that everybody would have to stand to let more people crowd in. Oh my and 9 hours yet. We in the front row stayed happily seated, occupying the space which would later hold our feet, and with our feet out into the street. The night dragged on. The gutter was filled with orange peels and food wrappers and the rain still poured. The police stood drippingly every 6 feet along the mile-long street. Our blanket dripped. Two policemen tried to wring it out for us. Newspaper boys came by selling papers with a picture of the queen's gown. Slowly the crowd was getting excited again. At 5:30 am the loud speakers were switched on and a very 'English' voice said, "Good morning, are you sitting comfortably?" and then proceeded to play symphonic music. Newsboys came by with later editions and there on the front page *was us*, sitting under papers, coats, blankets etc. The people on the Mall had made headlines! And still thousands of people walked past.

We heard shouts and a clumping sound. Down from the palace were marching the Queen's tall guards looking like tin soldiers. Red jackets, black trousers with huge round beaver hats set down to their eyes. Our hearts sank. If we had one of those in front of us we wouldn't see a thing. They went through much ceremony and then took their positions opposite us. We were still ok. Within an hour's time the Australian Navy marched under the arch. We chanted "We want a short one." They marched up and stopped. We were in real luck; flat hats, short and far apart. All was safe and 8 hours to go. After 4 hours of standing at attention in the rain, the shivering lieutenant shouted "Upp Hiz Eyq Eat," and still standing the Australians ate their sandwiches. We felt sorry for them. They were wearing summer uniforms and no rain coats and dare not relax.

Suddenly it began. Cars and coaches began to line up for the procession. In front of us were Nehru, Milan, St. Laurent, Kenzies...First closed cars, then coaches slowly went past. Beautifully dressed people wearing shining jewelry rode past and smiled at us. The costumes and colors were magnificent. Enthusiasm got higher and higher as Princess Margaret rode past. Bob stepped out with his camera. The Queen Mother smiled directly at us and the shutter snapped. To our left was the top of the gold carriage, and like a fairy story passing slowly in front of us, was the Queen and the Duke of Edinburgh waving and smiling. We forgot all about our wet clothes and stood in awe. Everything glittered and reflected as in the wet street we waved. We watched it pass, go through the arch and disappear and heard the shouting of the crowd move into the distance.

Then came the big question. We had seen the queen. Should we remain for five more hours, while she was being crowned in the Abbey, to see her again on the way back? Some people left – we stayed. The loud speaker kept us abreast with all the Abbey proceedings while we dropped off to sleep and then woke and then slept.

The Australian Navy still stood at attention, shivering. The white starch in their caps ran down their necks and faces and one man's black beard had turned white. The head officer finally marched to the end of the line, clicked his heels and wiped off the sailor's faces and necks with his hanky. The crowd cheered. Police collected hard candy and slipped it into the hands of the Navy but they weren't allowed to move their hands. Two young girls went along the line and popped candy into starch-covered mouths. No argument! We fell asleep and woke up to hear, "Now she is symbolically lifted to the throne," rain poured – symbolically.

Time passed and the procession came in sight again, this time much bigger. The Queen's 30,000 soldiers from all over the world wearing beautifully colored uniforms marched by carrying bayonets.

As far as the eye could see the bayonets glistened in the bright sun that decided to appear. Again the rulers of the world rode by, the counts and countesses, the Queen of Tonga, in her now famous rain-ignoring open carriage, the Queen Mother in white fur and Princess Margaret, the horse guards on beautiful black horses wearing blue jackets, silver armor and re-plumed helmets. Then the gray horses and again the Queen – this time wearing her crown, smiling at everyone. The procession was nearly over and we hadn't seen Churchill. Here came his black carriage but he was unhappy about something. He poked his big head out and shouted to the driver. At the next crossing he left the procession and turned off. It was over. We picked up our wet belongings and made our way through the millions to a subway. At the edge of town we raised our thumbs, and were back in Stratford-upon-Avon by 11 pm, and had seen all from a distance of 15 feet. Something we'll never forget.

Original watercolor by Vivian

Judy Garland

I just watched a documentary on Judy Garland's life which brought connections long forgotten. When I was 'little' - not sure what age, a few girlfriends and I climbed up a ladder fastened to the wall of the barbershop. It was a real trick to climb the ladder and push up the heavy lid to the attic. You held on to the ladder with one hand and Really Pushed to lift the big lid so it would fall open, and with a giant step, raise yourself into the attic by holding on to the rafters. We did it many afternoons.

It was a place not ever inhabited by parents. We played "Movie Stars." There was a huge trunk of 'stuff' we dressed up in and we gathered and pored over some old movie star magazines. No Idea Where They Came From. I always wanted to be Shirley Temple, but I was too tall and had straight hair, so I had to be Judy Garland. When it was time to come down, my mother would tap on the lid several times with a broom handle to let us know it was time to come down. We'd take turns carefully maneuvering ourselves one at a time back to Reality.

In the attic was the only time I smoked. We rolled my dad's cigarette papers around some stolen coffee grounds and nearly set the house on fire.

A few years later, a theater group traveled the Midwest called the Toby Players. I think they came once a week with a different play but the same characters. The whole town went, including my mother who later never went outside around Bogue, except out the back yard and of course, to the outdoor outhouse. Well one big deal was that jars of beans were placed in the front of the players. When we entered the hall, we were given a paper to guess how many beans were in each jar. At intermission, they pulled out the winning slips. All I really remember is sitting next to my mother and her saying, "I'm not going up even if I win. I'm not!" I wondered why she even entered the guessing game.

The second unknown is how I got chosen, asked, or PUSHED into being an intermission act, singing Judy Garland's "It Never Rains but What it Pours" and the "Wine, Women, and Song" both on the Accordion once and doing a chalk drawing to music another time. I do remember an evil girlfriend said, "I saw your pencil drawings." Then to others, "So she didn't make that up." It wasn't called 'bullying' then.

Many, many years later, another occasion occurred. I was visiting a close friend, an ex-student in Los Angeles. He was a top model and hoped to be a movie star soon. Judy Garland was drinking heavily and trying to quit. She stayed on his sofa one night. Months later I was again visiting him in New York. She called him from LA to help her. After her shows, it was such a letdown. To keep from drinking, she would call people randomly chosen from the phone book to chat.

I attended her last concert with my friend. At the end, he ran up the aisle with open arms shouting, "Judy, we love you!" She had tears and came home with us to sleep on the sofa.

John Gielgud

When I lived in Stratford-upon-Avon, England, I wished I had courage enough to get connected with the Theater Company, who at the time included Richard Burton, Sir Lawrence Olivier, Sir Michael Redgrave, Vivian Leigh, Alec Guinness, and many others sharing the stages at Stratford. We hitchhiked to London and saw the entire season several times. So many Big Names in English theater. Here's some little stories.

We lived with a friend from Scotland, next door to John Gielgud. Gielgud was rehearsing his one man show, Ages of Man. Our back gardens were connected by rose bushes. Every morning Gielgud would rise early and do his vocal exercises. We would sit on our side of the garden with coffee. He was rehearsing for Man of La Mancha, and we would listen as he went over each line trying different interpretations until he got it right. I mean Over and Over as he readied for the reading. I felt I could easily prompt him if he needed it. One day at lunch time I felt I had had enough of it, so I walked into the front garden. I glanced over to see him walking, looking very blank, immersed in thought. Around the corner came a lorry - LOUD. He kept walking and rehearsing lines. I grabbed him and pulled him aside so he wouldn't be hit.

He tipped his hat and said 'thank you' then continued his walk. Costuming was Huge for the season so I was asked one day at tea if I would be interested in helping produce 300 costumes. YES, one of my jobs was to sew a pocket inside King Lear's robe for the scales to weigh a 'pound of flesh.' I was thrilled!

During the opening performance, the costumers were asked to watch the stars for added details from the front row. When it came time for Gielgud to reach for the scales he pulled from the inside pocket - it wouldn't let loose. Ariel was dancing around him to cover the pocket problem. I was on the floor hiding from the too-small pocket mistake. He tugged and tugged. It wouldn't budge and wouldn't budge and finally he just ripped the pocket to retrieve the scales and continued. I floated away out of the theatre dying of embarrassment. I was told later that 'everything went fine.'

I also sewed a hook on his cape collar. Ariel went to say the line - his cue - and he went to open his cape and it wouldn't come, wouldn't come. He finally and firmly grabbed it and ripped it open.

Price Marden

He went to Florida Southern - Very quiet and had a stillness that was beautiful. He took one of my classes though he was an Art Major. I cast him in a Shakespeare play - no lines - just stood there in costume looking wonderful. He went to New York and I lost track of him until I saw his paintings at the Walker Art Center, and read that he taught Jackson Pollock and did enormous plain paintings with a thin line going through. He had one on a retreat with a religious man and painted with a twig.

He has two girls and built beautiful homes for them on a Greek island. When I was on tour, we stopped there years ago. The group stayed in the coffee shop drinking Turkish coffee. I wandered off to find their houses. I didn't, but I passed a building that had stacks of addresses and phone numbers, so I tried to look up their addresses. Of course, everything was in Greek. I stole some of the Big Book and carried it all over on the trip to bring home to George - of course he wasn't interested but could read it.

I forgot to mention, I had not paid any attention to the time and when I realized it, I RAN back to the port. They were just starting to lift the RAMP and LEAVE! I RAN, jumped on, and slid down. The group clapped. I would have had to take a once-a-week plane to the mainland at great expense!!!

Larry Rivers Cocktail Party

This followed a story about working as entertainment on the Arosa Sun and being invited to the captain's cabin. I had gained weight, so when the <u>short</u> captain insisted, I couldn't sit because my Chagall designed fabric/dress wouldn't bend.

Speaking of skintight dress or regained shape, I must tell you about our big London day. If I never go to another party, I have lived. We drove to London – Both had an appointment with our hairdressers. I haven't been to Raymond of London for 4 years, so it was special – in fact a Super Do – I was told I'm maturing beautifully – Rotten Swing! The fact that Mr. Bry did a wonderful job of cutting is a minor detail – the boss – Raymond, who just works on Vogue models came over, sat beside me, talked, then started experimenting with hair styles, hair pieces. In the middle of the procedure, he had me go put on my cocktail dress I was going to wear to save the hairdo. I was afraid to bend in it, so he said, "You stand, and I'll stand on the steps (he's 5 feet tall). Of course, the fun was all the society dames with their poodles with gold and pink collars, looking on enviously – didn't know I came from Bogue!

Now I must back up. William Scott designed some drapery material and had it woven of heavy linen. I saw it at his house and wanted to make it into a dress. He was amazed and excited. I made it (well I stood while Bob pinned it to my skin and then I sewed). Scott's gallery had heard and wanted me to come show it.

On to the cocktail party at London's leading art gallery to celebrate the opening of a Larry Rivers show (we bought one). Eighty guests in a small room with the paintings - some swinging from chains, pieces of sculpture and many waiters with champagne - where I had too many glasses – (the waiter was a flirt). I seem to get special attention by bartenders at all parties that keep refilling my glass.

The guests were Top Notch artists, collectors, newspaper men from all over including the Herald Tribune (he knew Walter Kerr, my college teacher), critics, photographers. We startled them with our entrance. I met 3 Sirs - Sir Walter Reed - art critic who has written 20 books including a blurb about Scott and the one our Tobey was in. Also Head of the Tate Gallery who had granted us the only permission ever given to take a child in a stroller through the gallery. The climax came when Mr. and Mrs. Scott arrived - the dress was a Huge Success. He told everyone proudly about it - "It's the best my art has ever been hung."

Birthday Gift of Hair Styling by Raymond Luis Estevez

I must tell you about my Christmas present from Bob. It's unbelievable. He caught a ride to London before Christmas with the Ramsey's and came back with my present - an appointment to have my hair styled, cut, and permed with Raymond, the classiest beautician in London and Paris. They have a HUGE staff, but Bob insisted that Raymond himself style my hair. Every month throughout England they have a beauty contest, and he styles the hair. He also brings his models to New York every three years for a style show. Oh, I was scared and excited. A thing like that would cost $50 in NY - here it was $18 for perms - everything. The experience was worth it. I felt like a queen.

Raymond and 3 assistants 'worked' on me for several hours. The weather was dry, so I got to sit under a dryer on their balcony overlooking a gorgeous park. The place was full of models, actresses, "Ladys" and their French poodles. The poodles sat and looked straight ahead - too snobby to acknowledge the other dogs or each other. Many customers conversed in French with 'their' beautician. I was a peasant. One Frenchman beautician came across the room and said in a thick accent, "Madam has beautiful eyes to emphasize." That was ME! I had to act like I was accustomed to that sort of thing. I asked 100 questions and learned a lot. It was amazing. I saw at least 25 women ranging from 40 - 90 and no two had the same hair style and all seemed to be 'right' for them. Some asked for a haircut, and they would just rearrange, others thought they needed a perm and ended up with one side reshaped. Women that looked like witches were made to look outstanding and classy. Everyone warned me they'd try to sell me lotions, facials but Raymond told me my hair was in perfect condition and needed none of those treatments.

He checked every angle of my face, had me walk, sit, stand, asked how tall my husband was, and when finished showed me several ways to comb my hair. Also, what to have future operators do for a perm. My perm is tight, not fuzzy, my hair is fluffy and although it's cut it looks much thicker than usual. No more spending hours combing and pinning. I've walked in the rain, fog, wind, and my hair stays in place because of the cut. We've taken pictures from every angle. Bob says I really do look like a model. It emphasizes my eyes and cheek bones and makes my glasses look good instead of extra. I don't know myself and I get lots of compliments.

Later, I went back to Raymond on several occasions. I went before our 3½ week hitch-hiking trip through Europe. Three men came over and whispered, "How many rides?" They knew Bob and I hitched from Stratford. When I went in, in preparation for the trip, I said I'd be in every kind of situation, even sleeping under a bridge. They smiled, looked around and said, "We shouldn't know that love."

I was there once with Katherine Hepburn. When they finished poring over her, she got up, ran her hands through her hair and in her nasal voice said, "Thanks guys," then someone brought her floor length fur coat. She slung it over one shoulder and swept down the curved steps to the exit below.

Drawing of Black Silk Dress

Let's see - I doubt I can keep it in order or even on the same topic to your question: "What is the story behind the Estevez sketch of you?" I'll try. I designed the dress to wear to a special occasion (if I turned up) on a trip by myself to NY City. Black silk with lace trim. I had more courage then and a waistline. I was staying on Long Island with Bob's mother. I'd dress for city shops and shows to attend all day and late night then take the train to Long Island where she lived.

One night walking from the train stop to her home, a man jumped out at me from a parked car I passed. I outran him (I could really run in those days). After that, after the last show, I tried going to a phone booth, fastening a cloth on all sides, and changing into something ugly to take the train back. An ex-student from Florida Southern named Richard Tatro (he was a second Richard Burton - looks, voice and pock-marked face) was living in a most elegant 'borrowed' apartment on Park Avenue. It was borrowed from the then famous designer Louis Estevez. Mrs.

Fusillo suggested I stay there where I'd be safe. Richard was insulted. We were so far apart we phoned each other from our bedrooms (this was before texting). We met in the kitchen which was stacked with dirty dishes. Fresh flowers were arranged for us daily.

Richard was doing underwear ads for Sears, and a porno film which he said was hard work, and drinking a coke upon billboards all over Europe. (I haven't forgotten the reason I'm writing.) Richard and I were invited to Estevez's High Fashion Show. I'd never been to one. Well, Richard and I were running down an alley jumping over bolts of fabric to get to the show - late. I was wearing gold fabric heels that I covered with black lace. I used bad glue and the lace was flapping loose. We had front row seats. Estevez held up the opening for us, we sat down, and he glared at us. The audience was all nervous buyers. We were on a different level - deciding whether we liked the buttons.

After the show I was shown the workrooms and told to choose any fabric I wanted. I chose black stretch which later became an evening gown I wore to Theatre of the Mind with the theme Paper, Packaging and Production. The Black Box Theatre was wrapped in paper and addressed to me, and I was given paper roses and photographed on the set.

Back to this story. After the show, Estevez also asked us to deliver loads of fur coats to Gloria Swanson's apartment. Even then he didn't have time or desire to pay attention to me. I was wearing a see-through knit top with gold pockets 'carefully placed' which appeared as a drawing in the next Women's Wear Daily as HIS DESIGN along with a review of the show.

Richard and I were taken in his limo out to the World's Fair where he was giving another fashion show. Gloria Swanson sat in front with a hat that had her trademark - a very high feather. Richard and I were in the back seat. Richard kept trying to tell Estevez what I had done. He ignored us - wasn't interested. We stopped at a nightclub - loud music - he sat opposite me and became very interested and said, "Let's go somewhere where we can talk."

It was a fun evening. He offered Richard and I tickets to a

special Broadway show that Richard Burton and Liz Taylor were reading scenes on a Monday. Monday was chosen because all Broadway shows were closed down and the movie star world could attend, and we would be in the audience. OK Ready...I Wore the Black Silk Dress. Richard and I were delivered to the theatre in Estevez's elegant convertible limo (it was written up in the NY Times as the only one in the city) and by his gorgeous black driver. We got much attention driving through Times Square and it started to sprinkle so he pulled onto a side street and put the top down.

Well, we arrived in front of the theater. The path was roped to hold back tourists trying to get a glimpse of the celebrities. Normally that's where I would have been. We sauntered in. In those days, I sort of looked like the famous model, Suzy Parker, if you weren't close. I heard someone say her name and, "That can't be Burton, he's in the show!!"

Well, we walked down the aisle to the 5th row. The theatre was filled with recognizable Broadway and movie stars. We sat down. I sat next to Zero Mostel. Another side note: At this time there was a show on in New York about fake tattoos and you get in by wearing one or more. Craig, another alum who became part of me through years of excitement and was a TOP MODEL at that time (another story), got a pasties tattoo of a black bull and placed it on my chest, so just the tail showed through the lace trim. Lauren Bacall started to sit behind me, leaned over and in her low voice said, "What the Hell is that?!" That evening performance is another story ending up at a theatre party with Burton and Liz. I was wearing The Black Dress. Estevez sketched and signed it and sent it to me.

Original Design
for a
tall Texan
like
Vivian Fusillo
by
Luis Estévez
(no copying please)

Andy Warhol

Craig was a top model and he insisted I needed a break and should come to New York City for a weekend. Andy Warhol was interested in using him for some project and Craig used that as an excuse to have me there.

This was at the Factory, a huge studio with shelving all around high up, filled with tape recordings - all for his films. We were there just a little while when a door opened and a woman I'd seen on some of his Huge Posters came in. She was Nude wearing only black heels and an ankle bracelet (I kept my attention on the ankle bracelet.) I forget her name, but she said she had an idea for a film. He said in his very quiet voice, "Get the camera ready, we'll shoot it." He paid NO attention to me.

Hairspray

Marc Shaiman - Music, Scott Wittman - Lyrics

I was visiting Craig in Hollywood. He decided I would like to visit two of his friends, Marc Shaiman, and Scott Wittman. I think he had created a flower garden for them, so we dropped in. They were very busy re-working their Broadway musical - HAIR-SPRAY. Craig suggested to Marc he should show me his studio. The walls were covered with framed awards he had won for his music. He ignored my oohing and aahing. He's a very quiet, plain Jewish boy - mostly Non-Verbal.

He went over to his piano and said to me, "Let me see you walk across the room." I started, and he created music on the piano as I walked. He said one word, "Beautiful," and we went to join Craig and Scott. Craig was the obvious entertainer to this quite short and tall couple.

The next day, Craig called them and said he wanted me to see the show, so they had front row seats for us - TOO CLOSE. Craig wore his Gold Lame Suit and I - it didn't matter what I wore. I really didn't like the show, but two of the lead women on their Big Number winked at Craig, and I guess gave him the sign to meet us afterwards. At intermission, we went to a theatre bar next door, and some woman was fawning and gushing over Craig and he got into a philosophical argument with her and almost missed the second half.

Years later Craig died. At his funeral were such a variety of people - street bums, Broadway stars who sang and played, his sister, his two boyfriends that had never met, and a man who he bought his illegal parrots from. He had an opera singer come to his apartment and train it to sing some opera numbers.

Craig and I had agreed long ago that if we didn't find anyone, we would live together AND not attend each other's funeral. Well, his roommate called and asked me to come. I was the only one who knew his college life. I flew in and stayed with Kim Schultz - three floors up and No Elevator. Before the funeral, I went to see his roommate. He had food and drink, and had all his rings displayed, and tossed a small container holding part of his 'cremation ashes' in my lap.

Well, after the service where I told college student stories, a group went to Mark and Scott's NY apartment. WOW - they had purchased several, maybe five apartments on the top floors and re-decorated them. The living room was so large they had three very long, white leather sofas with HUGE coffee tables and other stuff, like a corner to show movies and performances of Craig, etc. open to a kitchen and down a hall to at least 2 bedrooms and a bath-room. Two of the walls had floor to ceiling HUGE enlarged portraits of Craig. Beautiful lamps.

I mostly stayed by myself and remembered. The one (not live in) boyfriend came over and told me how much Craig loved me and my girls and was so glad I could come. And he had a huge enlargement of my Avedon photos. All this happened in one weekend, and I flew back to my job and the girls, to another style of living.

Horsey Stuff (Secretariat)

When I directed <u>Of Mice & Men</u>, the cast and I went to Nankivil Farms and stayed all night in the barn with the animals, which was a little 'too much reality' for me.

When I directed <u>Equus</u>, the cast gave me a present - beautifully wrapped. I got up very early and went out to the Nankivil Farm. I sat on the wooden fence where I could see the sun come up and opened the present. It was a photograph of beautiful horses. I felt something brush my shoulder. It was one of the horses looking over my shoulder. So, I shared my picture present with him.

Lance Belleville, a newspaper writer, came to see my play. He had to sit by the door in case he got a call that the famous racehorse Secretariat's sire was ready to be born, in which case he would have to escape during a high point of the play. He ended up being able to stay for the full show.

Days afterward, he invited Shari, Siobhan, and I to the farm to watch him take photographs for Life Magazine. He took one with both twins with a pony coming over the hill. I was hoping it would be in Life.

Encounter with the Pope

I know our neighbor Peggy travels with a priest friend once every few years and he arranges for her to see the Pope. In contrast, Rod and I were in Puerto Vallarta, and it happened, and I'll never know whether Rod planned the timing. We stayed at a motel, very simple with an enormous swimming pool.

Well, the Pope visited! In those days he didn't have to travel in a bullet-proof car. They had no army, so kids came from all over to stand, lining the street. And the Pope stayed at our motel! He had with him many Gorgeous Italian stewardesses and some other people including the man who traveled the world to find the perfect fabric for the Popes' Gowns.

Rod spent time flirting with the stewardesses in the pool and I had a wonderful time with the designer of the Pope's costumes. The radio wanted to interview the Pope, and Rod with his radio connection made sure we were in the radio station – after all, Rod was Catholic.

Meeting Shelley Winters

Craig had persuaded me to come to Hollywood where he lived - trying to 'get into the movies.' While there, his father died and he had to leave for Florida where he had lived. He left Hollywood to me, with instructions on what to do if drug dealers came by. I got my nerve (past talking to his neighbor who had just got out of prison) to go to the corner to get info about a bus to the 'main street.' Two guys were there and rather than tell me, they decided to go with me and show me where to get off the bus.

I was walking down the street when someone in a Big Black Limo shouted, "Hey Miss, you need a ride?" It was Richard Tatro, a past student from Florida Southern, along with Craig. He told me he was with Shelley Winters, ushering, companion, chauffeur. He insisted I join them for dinner AND come to her birthday party the next evening. We went for coffee, and it was time to pick her up. She was so amazing. We really hit it off - in fact she wanted to get rid of Richard but... We went to 'her' restaurant and sat at 'her' table. The next day in a gossip paper it said, "Who is the New Lady in Town?" She was peeking all around when Richard asked her what she was doing. Her answer - "Looking for Celebrities!"

We talked and talked. She was like a little girl. She asked if she came where I lived, would I let her take one of my acting classes. She loved my hair, dark eyes, and pale lips. She also talked about a time when she was dressed in a long formal, going to be presented on stage. When she arrived, there was a huge crowd as she stepped out of her limo. She suddenly had to go to the bathroom and peed right there!

Later, Richard picked me up and we went to her home for the party. I was Very Nervous. He was Very Calm. The rooms were packed with Big Name Movie Stars. He told me to mingle and left me. I talked to a few before I saw Paul Newman sitting on a chair, so I went over and sat by him for the evening.

Doing 'The Siobhan' at Hugh Hefner Party

The Wisconsin Music Theatre is progressing with plans. They still want me to direct but I'm not at all enthused. They have a promise of $20,000, 10 from Johnson's Wax and 5 at least from Mae West and that's another story. I got a present of white woolen stockings from her.

Chicago has become interesting with a few friends. I think you'd enjoy being with a wonderful guy - the FM program director. He's still heard over WGXR and does most of the recording for the Chicago Symphony. He has KLA speakers hanging from his elegant walls and the most marvelous sounding Hi-Fi, not to mention an unending record collection.

Hugh Hefner Playboy Group threw a big farewell party to celebrate the end of a photo shoot for October Playboy. They flew Craig in from New York. My expenses were paid for an overnight visit to Chicago. Siobhan has a special dance she does to the babysitter's guitar chords and it is so fun. It's imitated to where it's known as 'The Siobhan.' At the Playboy Club we had the spotlight thrown on us, so Craig and I did 'The Siobhan' and everyone copied until the entire floor was doing it. Several asked us what our dance was called. Craig said, "It's the Siobhan, everyone in New York is doing it."

Louise Nevelson Memories

An artist friend, John Paoletti, and I used to collect bric-a-brac from old, abandoned houses when I taught at Western Illinois University and send it to Louise Nevelson's New York gallery to create her 'wall art' that sold for thousands. I always wanted her HUGE jewelry and fabric she draped herself in. Hers was REAL, woven in Tibet - mine was fake.

I met her in her New York gallery and was invited to her little New York hideaway. It didn't happen. I never got to feel her wardrobe and jewelry. I could buy the 1-inch eyelashes that she wore. Bob and I were in her New York gallery - run by her son. Bob was talking business, I was watching her brilliant colored pet parrot pooping all over her wall of boxes she had painted white and called 'wedding.'

The phone rang. Her son turned in shock to us; it was a message from California. She had just drowned in her private swimming pool.

Hanes Hosiery Shot

Craig was hired to be in a Hanes stocking ad and insisted I come along. He was to play the piano while the model danced on top of it. He always did things to 'warm up' the photographer as he set up - to get a better photo.

Well, all was ready and the model for Hanes Hosiery DIDN'T SHOW. The photographer was very upset. By that time, we were friends. He looked at my legs (I was wearing hose). He said, "You've got great legs. If you can fit into these heels, climb up on the piano, we'll shoot it." Craig helped me up.

He shot lots of angles and at the end exclaimed, "That was Great!" It was very difficult because the shoes were too small. I never saw the ad.

AVEDON PHOTO SHOOT

Birthday Party at Two Million Dollar Farm (Redford Film)

Sunday was a Big Day in spite of my lack of energy and endless health problems. George was training a young pilot, and we were invited to his 11th birthday party on a farm outside of Arcadia. The mother pushes her young son into many interests. She's a very thin, unattractive woman with tattoos, wrist bands, MUCH ENERGY, endless bragging about "Hawk" - her son is dyslexic, very intelligent and doesn't talk or show any reaction. The husband is quiet, endlessly smiling and 'leaves it all to her' while he's a veterinarian.

The house is *old* with a strange extension. Floor, walls are old, weathered wood lacking paint. When I reached for a towel in the bathroom, I got a splinter in my nail. Hawkin's bedroom is filled wall to wall with his bed and a full-sized pool table. The other rooms - a put together of odd shapes and STUFF everywhere.

The people invited to the party - a group of six boys his age was dunking for apples. Yes, water splashing everywhere. The other guests were two couples at a card table paying NO attention to anyone. His piano teacher - I've never seen anyone who was so 'all over everywhere,' and another teacher. At a little larger table with 5 chairs were men who looked like they were out of a movie - wild hair and beards. I tried but no one spoke to George and me, and a scraggly woman who maybe belonged to one man. One finished eating and got up so George and I shared a chair.

The mother RAVED about her son Hawk's pilot teacher and took photos. She wanted Hawkins to take us on a tour of his interests, showing his activities. It was LONG up and down hills walking so I said (because of my knee) I'd watch out the window. Meanwhile, Hawkins went out on his own saying NOTHING. She insisted she'd get the New Van to take me around. I looked out and decided I could walk (a mistake) so we got every detail of info: His bees, which they ship to California to 'pollinate' (in the past he gave George a JAR of honey in which I found dead bees in the bottom), his potted flowers, the prairie grass and flowers, the ducks, the geese (he grabbed one to show me). I asked if it had a name and he said, "They don't need one." (The only time I heard his voice), a huge fish tank - he dug through and pulled out a ½ inch fish, chickens - I picked up a feather and said it might make a necklace. I'll probably get a box of feathers. He's sent brown eggs with feathers stuck to them to George in the past. He was allowed to join the other boys to go to the river with Big Traps and we got the van. The step up was too much for my replaced knee so I tried the other foot. I didn't have enough strength and hit my bone - a huge swelling - black and blue and HURT. I stayed in the van and George was shown her "business operation" - ENORMOUS. She has 17 workers - Big Business in sheep (wool sold through Amazon) - Goats, Horses, Cows, Tractors, Huge Bundles of Hay I saw from a distance. She was answering questions I managed to ask from the back seat of the van.

People left at different times - not speaking. She thanked them over and over - we finally managed to leave. I couldn't go back to the house after that, so I went to the Acoustic. A group of musicians got together. Among them was a 'professional' who yodels I've heard before. I asked him to yodel - WOW, he did.

Jerry Siem is an alum from long ago; his brother joined me listening. He said it was Jerry's birthday (65). He called and Jerry wanted to talk to me, so I went outdoors. He thanked me - said if it was not for me, he would never have graduated or been in that movie with Robert Redford or had that Big successful business and speaking internationally about fly fishing. Wow!

The Story Behind This

Years ago, Jerry was in my speech class (that's before the Speech people decided I didn't have training and stopped me from teaching it), AND he was in Theatre of the Mind. Well, he missed the Demonstration Speech assignment. He was very 'interested' in the world of fly fishing, so I suggested he prepare his speech to be delivered outdoors to a live audience - me. We traveled together through brush and weeds and arrived at a beautiful river stream. He set up his equipment and waded into the water. I sat on the beach. We got through it, and on the way home I saw some beautiful green plants and picked one for each of the speech department desks. It was marijuana! He now speaks all over the world and has a huge fishing business in Montana.

My Discovery - Josh Praaten

A very tall, very handsome student from the athletic department took my Oral Interp class as part of Gen Ed requirements. I had assigned a persuasive speech. He had not prepared but found a piece of blue paper, folded it and used it as a puppet for a hilarious puppet show/speech behind the desk. He had NO theatre experience but I cast him as Macbeth and with his strong good looks and powerful presence, he was great. A few years later he listed 'puppeteer' on his resume that helped him get his first professional acting role. He went on to become a star in movies and on Disney streaming and lives in Hollywood. At graduation, he cut out of line to come over and thank me for 'finding him.'

Winona Ryder Ad

In late December, I had read about it in the newspaper and dismissed it. Santha called me - a push to try for it. Shari said, "Something to do." George said, "Get out of your retirement cocoon."

The auditions were being held at Samson Hall on a very cold day. I wouldn't go with the college kids, so it was arranged for the audition to be at my house and set the time. I still hesitated.

The auditioner from San Francisco and her young assistant arrived - with equipment. The assistant told me I was 'loved in Winona' and, 'Hi from Lee.' We sat at the dining room table, and I talked. We got into thrift stores, and she forgot the time. So, I was handed a script - a waitress. (At my age of 92??) She held a microphone up to my face which I avoided by looking down. She read the three 'customer lines' and then I was to respond in three different moods.

She packed up quickly and took equipment to her car. The assistant gave me a paper with the details: rules, dates available, that I would get $750 if I got a role and more each time it was shown. She told me I was 'Really Good' and left.

A few days went by and they called all excited - I got through the first step. The woman had called from San Fran. Rachael set the date for a photographer from NYC to take my picture (another $150). He would come to the house. He and his assistant arrived with one camera. He took one look at the house and said he'd go out and get all the equipment - umbrella, lights, tripods, etc, etc. He is doing a book. I told him he could photograph anything but the paintings. He was SO excited he photographed me walking through the house and just sitting on the bed. As I walked around the house, he shot *many* pictures of me (different backgrounds). He also shot *many* pictures of just items and corners all around the house (for his book). We were in the bedroom, and after he shot my 50 rings and a door covered with necklaces, he said, "This light is good - I need more equipment for this." I started to *lie down* and wait for him. I said something funny, and He Shot the Picture and They Used It! I told them about George and the airport, so he scheduled the next day. They left saying they'd see me in January.

He and George had a great time. I went to the airport, and he wanted a photo of the two of us. George had told him of my directing experience, so he asked whether I wanted to direct the shots. NO!

So Many Phones Calls

Producers called to set up *another audition* at City Hall this time. No parking, so Shari drove me and waited below in the car. I had chosen to wear my latest thrift find - a brown and gold tailored jacket. I walked up three flights of stairs to where two women and a few men were waiting - all in work clothes and plaid shirts? Rachael asked me to sit with her at her desk filled with legal papers to sign. The two men were the mayor and a retired minister I had met at a weird book club - went into a room and then came out in seconds. A very pretty young blonde with LOTS of make-up came out and Rachael asked if I could go next because my daughter was waiting. Papers were filled out, but I didn't know my social security number. The blonde girl took me in and told me to stand in front of a large white sheet of paper (first time I'd done that since Bob took photos of me pregnant with Santha, etc, etc.) There was a standing camera very close to my face and a box for Skype on a nearby desk.

I was given a script with lines about mittens. A male voice (in California) interviewed me: Was I born in Winona? "No, Bogue, Kansas." "REALLY? Any hobbies?" "Well - painting, designing clothes." Did I make what I was wearing? "No, nothing that stiff." "Tell me about your ring." "From Russia, from a former student." "OK, let's do the script." I did.

The pretty girl was sitting all this time, leaning on one hand. After I finished she jumped up and said, "YES" and thanked me. I left, and went down to get my SS number from Shari. We had to get it from George!

A few days later, they called SO Excited - "You Won! You Won!" Someone called on dates for shooting a commercial with Winona Ryder! Monday, Tuesday, possibly Wednesday. Wardrobe called and went on and on. "Wear what's YOU." I gave her George's number to call. "Bring four outfits along." She would have some for me. My partner (an actor from Chicago) would wear an Alpaca vest. She went on and on. George told her I was a designer. She said to be sure I wore knit (like mittens) or maybe not necessary - but if in case. On and on....

Other calls. I was to be at Wesley Church dressed in my favorite, in full make-up at 4 AM Tuesday for filming at 8 am. *What had I gotten into?* As a lifelong director and theatre professor, I was really only interested in the production and how it was done.

Monday Night: George was asleep with an hour to go before his flight. I walked into the bathroom for one of my many nightly trips. I reached for the toilet paper and my left arm dropped limp. My first thought was, 'I'll never sew again.' I hesitated, but walked into the bedroom and said, "I hate to wake you, but look what happened to my arm." Several times each night, half asleep he says, "Are you alright?" and goes back to sleep after my 'Ok.' He threw off the covers, jumped up and said, "Get dressed - we're going to the hospital." He phoned the hospital to be ready. "We're coming." I grabbed my shoes and coat. He (as always) said, "Be careful going down the steps."

Through red lights etc, etc. he got us there. They weren't busy. Quickly, George had papers filled out. He knew there was little time - I needed to be treated within an hour and it was 45 minutes gone already. I was ushered into a special room and two doctors and two nurses were moving quickly. George called Shari and Siobhan. As they prepared me, I was told Peter and Brooke (in her PJ's) were in the lobby. Shari said she'd contact Santha. Time was of the utmost importance.

Someone mentioned flying me to Mayo. George knows the plane and the three pilots. He said, "There's not enough equipment on board." He told me I'd go by ambulance, and he would be right behind me. Siobhan would ride in the front seat.

An earlier memory - I was in New York visiting Kim and got up too fast and fell and hit my head on her marble windowsill. We discussed if I was ok. Kim called George who said, "Get an ambulance." I said, "Not with red lights and sirens!" I had a concussion and was bleeding. Skipping all the details, Siobhan flew from Winona to New York to be with me and take the train back. Our 2nd time in an ambulance but very different roads and people!!

I was all hooked up and forgot about my arm. The operator had been all over the world - we talked about buildings, people. Now and then the machine growled, and he quietly fixed it. A little over halfway there I could MOVE ONE FINGER. George met us. I was given many needles and lifted and swung from sheets to testing machines and then taken down halls with Wonderful New Artwork. Lots of attentive nurses. Bed pan - ugh. I slept through the night - first time in years. Lots of talk - what could I eat, etc, etc. All Hooked Up.

My day nurse was Wonderful. She looked like Monica and had an English accent (from North Dakota). I've had trouble swallowing without choking so George had arranged for that to be tested - another ride to more machines. They photographed me eating and drinking. It's 'Age and Dryness.' My esophagus had shrunk and slipped forward. "EAT SOFT FOOD." (Big deal with the kitchen.) I'm to spray my throat and eat soft food every two hours.

George and the doctor had long intellectual talks about what to do to prevent this happening again - the doctor was in heaven to talk to an intelligent man. Somebody (Shari) phoned to cancel the Winona Ryder commercial. Back and forth, and finally they said they'd postpone it until Wednesday - hoping. Tuesday came

128

and I was wobbly, sore and purple from being jabbed, but much better and would be let out Tuesday pm.

Phone call - I was still in the commercial! They would adjust the schedule. Tuesday - lots of prep to go home. George and the doctor talked so long I thought I wouldn't make it, but got back about 7 pm Tuesday night. Shari and Brooke came over and went through a stack of clothes about 2 feet high saying, "This is You; this isn't You." I was SO TIRED.

I remembered a knit (Eskimo/Africa) skirt I had in the basement - hadn't seen for 60 years. Good Colors. Shari went down and found it. I moved the waist up and rolled it around a snake bracelet Rod bought me years ago and created a blouse. I didn't mention it - there were many calls to Shari. I was told I'd be sitting... "wear comfortable shoes,"... "will be seen from the waist up." Shari gave me ALL the instructions. Be dressed in make-up at 4:00 am to go for the shooting. I slept a bit.

At 3:30 Siobhan arrived all made up in case she got in to help me, and carried the stack of extra clothes that were 'me,' in case wardrobe didn't like my choices. Got me into her car and went to Wesley Church. There were big trucks all over, filled with electrical and filming equipment. Back up to Mayo - I must tell you about my special nurse from Russia that adopted me. In between doctors and nurses, food, bathrooms, etc, a short, stout, determined woman came in and TOOK CHARGE. The curtains were closed so I could rest. She *shoved* them open and entered with a young assistant. I would guess she was 55 and she sat on my bed with me and said: 1) "You're a good person, I can tell." 2) "Is that a wig?" (No) 3) "I'm going to comb your hair." (The young nurse standing behind just shook her head.) 4) George walked in - she grabbed and hugged him - to his surprise. I asked her - she'd been at Mayo 20 years and was from Russia - she couldn't believe I couldn't speak Russian.

The day I was to go home that late afternoon when I needed to get out to rest before the filming - she came in. "No shower. But you can't go home smelling." She yanked the curtain closed, told me to take off my clothes, grabbed a bucket of water and gave me a *standing bath* and said, "That's how it should be," and left.

Now for the Real Story

Siobhan ushered me into the church basement in a room with long tables and all the hopefuls filling out legal papers, a table with Man in Charge calling out orders. Crazy looking wardrobe lady handing out clothes for people to put on. We sat. It was too much for Sio to fill out both sets of legal papers - a girl from the Co-op came over and filled out mine. Sio called Shari to come - she might get in. They arrived. Man called out - All 'hopefuls' wouldn't be needed. Shari and Brooke went home. "Shooting will begin at 8 am." Man called out, "Viv," and said, "Good - you're fine." Time to go into the room for filming. Sio helped me. Man said, "Are you Vivian's daughter?" Yes - OK - Together we went into the main filming room. This is the set up. The room was filled with stands with local business' products displayed and an 'extra' standing behind me.

Everything was in its place. The crews were nervous; Lots of talking. The stand-in (Ryder's double), a girl with same length/style black-dyed hair and white face and NO expression, with a Chicago actress, walked down the hall past Sio and toward our mitten table several times to check out everything. Then we were to 'try' the 5 lines (about mittens). They had given all the lines to the actor from Chicago (I would have never cast him) because they didn't know whether I would even make it. She then turned and looked at the mayor sitting in a chair on the side of the stage, and she pointed and said, "Oh look, there's the mayor." Much too much expression so they did it several times.

The director came to our table followed by cameras and sound. The *camera broke* so two crew members rushed to fix it. They stopped at our table and my Chicago actor partner said the 5 lines about mittens and I was the last word (I can't remember what). He stood - I sat. The director got an idea and said, "Again, only this time YOU (me) say 'the word' and then look at the camera and say, 'I just made that up.' OH, the word was 'Relax.'

The camera and trailer pusher and sound man then came down that aisle past the mayor and 8 stands on either side - past Julie's paintings including one of me on a big easel and stopped by two musicians who played a piece several times - one was a retired minister I met at a weird book club I went to twice. They rolled past all the other stands and to a table with three large puppets. The boy who made them had the puppets talk and we thought the filming was over. Instead, we were told that it was all a rehearsal and we'd go to make-up, but since there was nothing else to set up, everyone talked. I looked up and saw Ryder talking to the director so 'Quiet Everyone.' Then she looked at me and said, "May I take your picture?" They handed her a camera - Flash - that was done twice.

Sio came in the room and sort of helped me up to look at the other stands then found two chairs by Judy's paintings. We sat. The puppeteer came running up So Excited and said, "I was one of the boys in your last Peter Pan." A woman came up and sat on the floor and said she was so happy to meet me. She worked on Grumpy Old Men and was a friend of the author and couldn't wait to tell him she met me, and heard I go to the Acoustic daily etc, etc. Judy wanted a picture with me. Then Sio said, "We have to go back to your table." I did and sat.

A make-up man was talking and putting make-up on my partner. I said, "I want my nose shorter." He said, "You're beautiful the way you are. I don't have that expensive make-up," but he sprayed me.

Because of my years as a director, I was very interested and watched the whole process and organization. The 'extras' were to go to their stands. My partner and I were to go to the table (covered with Winona Knits mittens) facing towards Winona Ryder's entrance. I was the first to be greeted by her. A large number of crew members were in position and others 'acting important' - I noticed a division between the two groups.

A large number of crew members were in their position and many others - a very nervous crew 'Ready.' At one time it was announced 'a break.' Siobhan was at the door to the hall, and I went to her. I realized I was to go into a room with all the SOUND crew. A young man came to me - I said, "Why aren't you acting important?" He said he had not earned it - jobs were so scarce. He took out a heavy microphone and untwisted wires and was hesitant to put it down my blouse, so I held the neck open, and he lowered it - will it get caught along the way? The man in the recording room shouted, "Places." My sound man looked desperate. I raised my arms and said, "Get it." He did, and I took my place sitting (with comfortable shoes) behind the Winona Knits table ready 'to greet Winona Ryder.'

The director came by, followed by the cameraman on a cart

pushed by someone (how do you audition for *that* job?), followed by 'my' sound man holding the mic and walking formally - not even a side glance to me. We got in our stand and sat behind the table; cameras moved in behind us to 'add background.' Now it was over.

Go to get my extra clothes from wardrobe. A couple of men said they'd heard about me and hoped to meet me and 9 hours after we had arrived, went to Acoustic for soup - *EXHAUSTED!*

Inspiration for Grumpy Old Men

I became aware of a newly released movie that had been shot in nearby locations, including Wabasha. A former student had written it - called Grumpy Old Men. No clue. It was apparently an instant smash hit.

Somehow I became aware that the movie (written by former WSU student Mark Steven Johnson, now a producer in Hollywood) was (loosely) based on me! The lead actress, Ann-Margret, played a 'free spirited' professor at Winona State. As word spread, I became identified as the inspiration for the Big Movie. At first I thought it all rather silly, but realized that was not how the rest of the world felt.

I was interviewed by CBS for a fill-in piece during a nationally telecast WSU game - a super high energy blonde woman came to my home, with many lights and microphones set up - interviewed for 6 hours (which they cut down to 4 minutes for airing). Completely uninterested in any of my stories of teaching or 100+

plays I directed - ONLY wanted to know the 'story' behind the now infamous movie.

I was part of the annual Grumpy Old Men Days celebration in Wabasha, MN. I sat in an ice fishing shack with Miss Minnesota and signed autographs. I wore a big floppy hat and rode in the back of a pick-up truck with Jon Bernadot serenading on guitar for a big parade around the main street.

An article in the Star Tribune featured side by side photos of me and Ann-Margret with a big write up. The whole thing was very strange and amazing.

Part Four

VIGNETTES

Ferris Wheel

I was visiting Craig in Hollywood while he was filming a Woody Allen film. When he finished, he needed to escape so we decided to hitchhike to Tijuana. We got on the road and were immediately picked up by the Head of Make-Up for his film! We got through the border, said goodbye to our driver who went all the way, and Craig wanted to take me to the circus. It was unlike any I had seen before. There was a merry-go-round but NO giraffe - just all ugly animals, frightening with blood dripping from the animal they were eating, and terrible color - even the music was harsh. I refused to go on the ride. I remember riding on a giraffe in Kansas, in New York in Central Park, in London, in Paris, and in Canada. This was different. So, we went to the Ferris Wheel. I was a bit hesitant because it creaked and looked like it was held together with toothpicks, but Craig insisted. I was REALLY HOT. He paid and we went for our next adventure.

The carny operator was like I remember as a kid - scruffy, teeth missing, wild dirty hair. Recently, the carny people had been clean shaven and read books while waiting. NOT RIGHT! He opened the gate and did a double take like he knew me. Probably an ex-student! We sat down, he shut the gate, and we started up. We slowly moved with some swinging and lots of creeks in the machinery and when we got to the top - we STOPPED. Probably to let new passengers on, we thought. We stayed there a *long* time and finally both said at the same time, "IT'S BROKEN." Well, the 1st hour at the very TOP we told stories and ate the lunch Craig had packed for later. The 2nd hour, we tried to name all good things. I said I had lost ten pounds from sweat and asked, "What time does the sun set?" The 3rd hour we decided we'd be there the rest of our lives, slowly swinging back and forth and melting. Craig said, "This is the closest I'll get to heaven." I was thinking HELL.

World's Largest Junkyard

I was teaching at Western Illinois University. It was a day without classes or rehearsals. The girls were all well and in school, SO I gathered together some theatre and art students and a photographer friend, and we met at the theatre. It was to be an Art Experiment, so everyone put on white face make-up with black eyes, nostrils and lips, and climbed into our various transportation. I led in our convertible, top down, with the photographer and equipment and we headed for the World's Largest Junkyard.

When we arrived, we couldn't believe it - miles of broken-down buses carefully lined up, and taxis and cars of every make and color, etc. All excited, we rushed through the gate, and everyone scattered and climbed around to get ideas. I had six students get in an old school bus with broken windows and look out while the photographer set up the shot. He had forgotten something, so I turned to go back to my car and came face to face with a very short, stout, fat man who said, "I called the sheriff and if you're not out of here in 10 minutes you'll be in jail." I turned around and all the students had all run and hid, so it was just me and I'm almost 6 feet and he's about 5. And I have a white face with black eyes, nostrils and lips looking down on him, but I began... I said how Rare and Beautiful his entire field was and did he know there was a big move in the art world called Junk Sculpture? "In fact, the Museum of Modern Art in NYC just had an exhibition of it." He just looked at me and I went on, "Did you know that an artist called Stankiewicz had become famous with his Junk Sculpture that sold for a Huge Price?" So far, no reaction so I went on, "If he knew of this Wonderful Collection, he'd want to meet you." Pause. He said, "I know Stankiewicz. He was here last month to get his supplies. I was invited to his New York opening." "Oh!" "This is private property, and you need to get permission to be here, so you'd better go before the sheriff gets here!" And we did.

Making a Film with Craig

We (the art pop painter plus an Andy Warhol assistant) have begun to film an art film on one camera. The experience is just as great as the New York photography sessions and blow up. The results so far are strangely beautiful. Craig, my drama student from Florida turned special friend and America's top male model, came to visit for a week. He was so great with the kids. The house seemed to have no problems, and all fell right in line. I was relaxed and had so much fun.

On the weekend we left campus with vans, convertibles, cameras, make up, and a group of selected people for their strange faces all dressed in black and white. We drove to a nearby town that would have cost MGM a million dollars to build up the atmosphere. Everyone got in clown white with black eyes and lips, and after a bit of public relation work with the local untouched people, we began shooting movies and stills, black and white and color and sepia.

Craig has even more of a chiseled face than mine. The two of us did several scenes. Wish I had one of the stills. We did lots of shots in a marvelous old pool hall, a dance up on a balcony with back lighting through splintered boards, a broken window and a hole in the roof, a love scene in the corner of a dirty, broken, splintered building whose entire wall of plaster tumbled down on me as I slid down the wall. We found a mountain - as big as a building - made of corn cobs and the two of us did a running, jumping, and standing still with a little 'humph' thrown in while two photographers ran around shooting. Some of the shots are fantastic. Have you ever tried running or riding a bicycle through corn cobs for exercise? I could go on forever telling details about each weekend of shooting. We found a Fountain Green that consists of a few houses, three main stores, and a huge farm completely full of broken, smashed, wrecked cars, buses, and trucks. We got lots of good shots, plus a big coil from a truck that makes an excellent record holder or a springy chair to shoot guests through the door.

Another weekend was unbelievable. We found a deserted house with beautiful furniture. Every corner was a work of art for filming. If we can find time to do some good editing this summer, it should be a fantastic film.

Snow Day

This is the first day in months – maybe a year – I've been in the house ALL DAY. It was exciting to have Santha drop off books and pick up more writings to type and tell me of her adventures skating and cross-country skiing on her break at work. I'm looking out at the pretty snow and thinking, "I wonder if I can still make snow angels?"

All my furniture and window ledges are filled with memories and stories. I just found a basket filled with tiny dolls, the seven dwarves, but there are eight!? Where to put them? They need show time.

I'm drinking hot chocolate and remembering the hot chocolate shoppe in London. I miss my two hours each day with people at the Acoustic Café – writing stories and meeting alums telling me what I said and did, and wore back then – I want to believe but....

Last night was the first night for weeks/months I didn't have nightmares about my funeral. I think it was brought about by the stories and past adventures I'm remembering and writing about. And my birthday is coming up. How could that be? I'm only 40. How could I have three beautiful girls OVER 50, and 45 years since my first day with George? It had been years since Bob had left us, but I still hadn't recovered and didn't know how to go on a 'date.' George was in charge of the college union (pre-doctorate degree and aviation world). I didn't know how to have a formal date or what to do with the girls. We were living in a house I had rented by phone from Hollywood. I was visiting an alum. The upstairs was a playground for the girls. I somehow got a babysitter and 'hid' them upstairs and hoped for the best. First thing George said when he came in was, "Where are the girls?" I was a little upset. He was only interested in them. All these 45 years he has remained so caring, and oftentimes too worried about them.

Our first date AND my 92nd birthday is too much in February to handle. I gotta get outdoors and down to the Acoustic. Oh, I just heard the mail woman......I hope....

Walker Art Center Opening

I went to the Walker Art Center gallery opening. The room was packed with people wearing every possible style of clothing. The outstanding that sticks in my mind were five beautifully built suntanned boys, swishing about in white shorts and pink T-shirts saying - something. For whatever reason, I can't remember, I wore a creation of rust velvet floor length gown cut on the bias. I had not rehearsed my walk in it so as I sauntered from artwork to artwork, the bias cut 'backless' dress slowly moved around my body so the backless back attempted to end up in front! Each time this happened I hid behind a large Picasso sculpture and tugged it back into place. A friendly gentleman came up to me and said, "You're having a hell of a time, aren't you?"

Someone - a former student - brought in a huge stack of gorgeous colored T-shirts with Picasso's signature placed boldly across the front. They were to be sold as souvenirs. Just then Picasso's daughter walked in, saw the shirts, and ordered them to be BURNED. Walker didn't have permission to print these. My student, following her orders, took the T-shirts out back and BURNED THEM. She didn't even save one for me!!

TOTM - Paper and Packaging

Theatre of the Mind scripts are in and casting complete, and now the billions of details begin. The theme is FOOD. We have great ideas - hopefully programs on paper plates, costumes may be garbage bags, tickets are seed packets to be planted and we start by making stone soup and end with EATING, and afterward the audience finds the cast doing dishes in the lobby.

When we finally put all our ideas together:

The Lobby

We hung George's PhD dissertation off the balcony. We had collected thousands of papers that school kids have to take home, and students in paper dresses continually handed these to the incoming audience. The entire main entrance was wrapped and addressed to me. I wore a black dress and had a big paper corsage.

Once the audience got into the Black Box Theatre through the back door, they were hit by all the stage lights and a loud mechanical sound.

The Show

The set was a series of platforms. The door at the back, a mistake made by the architect to go into the main theatre, was used to project all religions on the opening. The costumes were all paper. We opened by worshiping and ended by walking all over the set. We had the audience do origami. Each number had to do with paper, and the paper was *left on the stage.*

We had to clean it all up each time for the second show.

Fashion

Fabric is a vehicle for looking at humans. I'm interested in
packaging and presentation.

What can fabric do beyond what it appears to be?

The Saturday fashion shows. What is its essence? How can I
extract something pertinent for me?

The artist must shape, select and co-ordinate forms to precisely
project the meaning he wishes to convey.

I cannot control how I am perceived; I can only control how
I am presented.

Magical Leaves

I felt beautiful today. I had on a new dress - cross between linen and burlap, heavy with off-white flowers trimmed with just enough woolen French lace.... short and swinging with lace framing the legs...the brown curled wig with a lace ribbon... false eyelashes ...but that wasn't it....

I was Magic....

There was a hush when Santha and I passed groups on our way to school...I saw several heads in windows...looking. When I walked into class there was a vacuum that all the students tumbled into. After class I ran to the car and took the TV to the downtown repair man and told him it's his fault. He looked, then asked, "Do you live here?" I left so he could work.

Outside the wind was building and cold...I thought of friends who have money...all the right things. I thought of all the very special moments I've had with lots of individuals lately.

I ran to the car and drove to the gas station to check a low tire and leave the car because I heard the voice of a warm close friend who says on the phone late at night, "I worry about you, hon." The men in the gas station were confused by me and talked ever so gently. I left the car with them.

I began to walk...then run the three blocks home, as the wind whirled my skirts high and back again. I passed the football field and the Coach shouted, "How's my good lookin' baby?" And then...

Magic Stuff...

....the wind banged a door across the street open and shut.....there was nothing....and then...

Thousands of dried autumn leaves whirled all around me, made circles around my feet and danced off in beautiful patterns. I followed them and knew they knew they were leading me in our secret way. They hopped on one stem for a whole block and then a group came swirling down to hop with the others.

I was blown to Main Street where a car stopped. It was my

newly acquired elegant elderly friend...ex-Hungarian Diplomat... with beautifully expressive gloved hands, he waved, rolled the window down and said, "You are the Goddess of the Dancing Leaves."

I got to my mailbox, then the refrigerator and grabbed a hunk of cheese, slurped cucumbers in sour cream that dripped down to my elbows and climbed in bed for a quick rest before it was time to pick up the girls and then to listen to each of them all together shout at me, "Oh Momie, you know what happened to me today?"

Twins' Missing Coats

We were living in Winona – the girls were little – I decided they should wear their velvet dresses, white stockings and Mary Jane shoes, and we'd all go to a concert – in Lacrosse. I had made the twins coats of giraffe designed fake fur – so beautiful. We hung them on the coat rack in the hall. When we came out – They Were Gone!! We called the police. I described the coats. He said, shocked, "Real giraffe?!" We went home sad. The next day the police found two little boys wearing them – playing in a yard.

Santha's First Haircut

Letter to Helen Fusillo from VF in Stratford, England

The card read: Monsieur Raymond presents his compliments to Miss Santha Fusillo and desires to confirm the appointment with Miss June on Wednesday, January 2nd, 1963.

Santha had her first haircut, and what an occasion. We were all there at England's most fashionable hair stylist, Raymond. I was of course nervous whether it would work or whether she might destroy the atmosphere of elegant chandeliers and cupid angels hanging from wires and dashing young pointed-toed men, but she was a real lady.

Miss June, the manageress, took her in another room to get an apron and then she sat on my lap, watched herself in the mirror, and the cutting began. Miss June, after a few snips said,

"Oooh," and Santha flashed a big smile and 'Ooohed' back. She spied a huge stage ring on Miss June's hand and in her own private language asked for it. The wish was granted, and she sat with her tiny index finger held straight in the air with the enormous ring on it. Daddy took a couple of pictures. The apron was removed, and she looked so chunky headed and cute. She was put down and headed fast down the center aisle and around a corner, shrieking, before daddy could catch up.

While I had my hair cut, she sat quietly oohing and then began to sing. Miss June said she was so good. I said, "Yes, until her fussy period." "When is that?" "In about ten minutes." Oh! - so Miss June stopped snipping, raised her voice and said, "Mr. Charles, would you get the young lady a biscuit?" Two were brought out on a pretty napkin and plate, but while she munched, Bob discovered somewhere she had misplaced her own Ruby Ring, a big ring she loves to wear that came out of a puzzle. Bob and Santha started to look. Miss June spoke to her assistant, "Mr. Ralph, would you help look for the little lady's ring?" A few minutes later, Mr. Ralph came to me and said, "It's alright Madam, we've found the ring." No charge for Santha's cut. She let out a big hiccup, said "Bye-Bye" and we went out into the blizzard weather.

At the moment, England is coming to a standstill. Santha is wearing my fur hat, Bob's underwear around her neck, his socks for gloves, my purse and high heels - some sight! We call her Fagan.

Love,
    Viv

Santha — Phelps School - Grade 2

A Muslim woman in a bourka – long veil – walks past a family planning sign in Delhi. Few women wearing veils go to clinics for birth control. Answer – if women would remove their veils they could see the warning poster – OK?

I misread – accepting nomination for Conservation and Beauty in America – thought it said nomination for *Conversation* and Beauty – more interesting. I just went over to the Lab School to give Santha a message – the teacher who is of retirement age, has curly gray hair, pretty, turned up nose, twinkly eyes, excellent taste in make–up and clothes – Chipper! Grabbed me and jumped up and down and ran to the far wall of the huge class-room and pointed to the huge poster – Neat printing on a big, green paper was Santha's latest poem:

My Lollipop

I like my lollipop big and round, I cannot drop it
  on the ground
And that yummy chocolate in the middle, I'm glad
  it's not ice cream brittle
I like my lollipop big and round, It is greener than
  the grass on the ground

— BY SANTHA

Santha and I went past the music room, and the teacher grabbed me and told me of Santha's creative mind. She's written two beautiful little songs and the teacher is going to mark down the music and teach it to the class this week.

A Song
  The lazy daisy sitting in the Spring
  Not knowing what he was doing
  But along came a bee and stung him on the wing
  And that was the end of the poor little thing

Eating

Whenever 'company came,' which wasn't often because I had no time, the girls were normal in that they all tried to 'show off.' I

159

didn't want to be a cranky mother or give them 'the eye,' so I thought if there was a way, I could hook up a 'gentle shock' under the table so when I pushed the right button they'd get the point.

I had a Kansas City banker friend that drove miles to see us on weekends. Actually, I think the intrigue was because he was in a whole world he didn't know at all. The three little girls and I, while teaching and trying to make life keep going on our own in a rented house, were far below his level.

He sometimes brought a huge bag of fried chicken and cold drinks. We never had this on our own so the girls said he must be really rich. One weekend he wanted to take us all to a restaurant for breakfast. The twins didn't know what to do with the menu, but Santha ordered the most expensive - Steak!

The president of the college came over to the house. The twins were out, Santha was home and wanted to take over the entertainment. I went into the kitchen to get the only pie I'd made in years to serve, and she said, "Am I supposed to stay here and entertain the Pres?" He was delighted with her – I wasn't.

A friend from a previous university where I had taught – a bachelor who probably planned to remain that way – came to Winona over Thanksgiving to visit. We had the worst blizzard I had ever encountered. My VW was parked almost up to the windows in snow and not able to move. I had cooked a small turkey and 'stuff' and set the table pretty. I'm better at that than cooking. Both the twins became very ill while I was setting the table. He sat on the sofa holding the two sick little girls. When I came to rescue him, he said, "Is this the worst thing about marriage?"

Our first Christmas 'on our own' in Winona, a friend invited the girls and I for dinner. The dining table was huge with a grand tablecloth of blue. The high-backed chairs were upholstered in the same blue velvet. We arrived and drifted among the various people – all men but the hostess. She brought four platters with a turkey, a goose, and other meats. As we started to eat, each of 'the guys' described in detail how they had killed their animal. I completely lost my appetite.

Wardrobe Malfunction

After Ali Baba (third time), I went into my Theatre Appreciation class (with nerves because of six bad students). Zed had delivered the rest of the exam he forgot to copy. George went to get our new Dean to look in to see the kids at Ali Baba. Zed sat in a chair outside my classroom. I went before the class and felt the elastic give way to my ballooned Ali Baba-style silk pants made from a parachute. I had created a new top to go with the pants made years ago. The narrow elastic was rotten and stretched. I grabbed the sides, hoping the top would look draped, left the room, and told Zed. He said, "What are you going to do?" I headed for the women's restroom, pulled the elastic (now like a string) tight, tied it, and hurried back to supervise the test. Whee!

A Music Publisher & a Former Student Reconnection

Langford was a lawyer here in town who lived two blocks from us on Wilson. I'd heard of him and actually seen him when the girls and I went to a restaurant - that no longer exists - once a week for an 'outing' when we first moved here.

WELL...

Kahn - Father of Don Kahn - a nationally known music publisher who used local company Hal Leonard - was in Winona on a business trip and Langford arranged a party. When I met Langford 47 years later, I asked him why I was invited. He said, "You were the most exciting woman in town, and I was showing off." (No one ever knows how I really feel.)

ANYWAY...

I had something planned for the girls and arrived late. This little Jewish man made a big deal flirting with me. I asked for the bathroom and HID for a while, then went home. The exciting part was in the bathroom was a Beautiful Marble Bathtub. It had been carved in Italy.

Langford told me a young black kid named Stephan Bradley, who had been a dancer in TOTM, lived with him. He thanked me for all I did for him. He now lives near Langford and is very successful. He asked for my email.

Later I got an email from him, and this is what he said: "I still remember our first meeting during registration. You told a frightened young college student to trust you and I did. The rest was three years of Children's Theatre and a host of dance productions in Theatre of the Mind. Finally graduated in 1972. All this is to say, "Thank You!"

Acoustic Deli Group

I collect all kinds and ages of people and compliments during my Acoustic time. Today topped them all. Three rough looking guys (that doesn't begin to describe them) sat at a nearby booth. I glanced at them when looking for an empty booth - actually MY booth.

A short, black guy with beautiful teeth and a big smile looked up at me!

I found an empty booth and started to sit down, when my booth emptied, so I picked up my stuff and crossed past them to sit in my booth. As soon as I "got located," one of the men came to my booth. Let's see - how to describe him. Tall - well built (he was wearing old, ragged overalls). He had NO TEETH. He had a beautiful voice and excellent 'speech' - 50ish. He came to my booth to thank me for all I had done for him. He was a disaster. His wife divorced him, and he decided to enroll in Intro to Theatre at WSU. He said, "You were so kind to let me be on the light crew of James and the Giant Peach." The first one was 40 some years ago. He said he turned the lights off too soon and felt so bad. He came to apologize, and he said I told him that everyone makes mistakes. He thanked me for so many ways I helped him. While he was talking, the smiling guy was standing behind him and said, "Sam told me to tell you HI!" (Sam is Santha, my oldest daughter - now I am really confused.) While smiley was talking, Barry went to the counter and borrowed paper and pen and then handed me this note: ANYTIME YOU NEED A HELPIN' HAND DON'T HESITATE TO CALL ME - BARRY SANDS.

Acoustic Encounter – Imaginary Encounter

There's a fellow who comes in to the Acoustic every day - very average looking and dressing, maybe jeans, jacket, and cap, 40ish, slight beard but on him almost not noticeable. He never speaks to anyone or has any expression on his face or body.

Today I decided I'd get acquainted - go to his booth - if we're going to be here every day at the same time. So, I got out of my booth and started over to his, and was amazed. He was quietly talking to an imaginary person sitting opposite him! He was laughing and gesturing, and had a charm and personality like I've never seen. He was eating a dish of ice cream, and talking, smiling and gesturing to his friend.

He got up to leave, went to his car - with his friend - crossed the ice to open the door - for his friend - then got into the driver's seat and, still laughing, drove off. I'd like to meet his friend if he appears again!

Artist at my Booth

I was reading and enjoying my daily AP and reading and marking all the events I wanted to go to (and probably won't),

166

when out of the corner of my eye there was a large stomach hanging over the table, and a voice said, "Am I bothering you?" It was the artist taking photos of his painting at the Acoustic.

Sex Story

My daily hour lunch at Acoustic Cafe is to be with college kids, waiters, alums from years ago, some people I don't remember ever meeting, or just people walking. This day was most unusual - a completely different scene. I sat in 'my booth,' kitty corner from a young Japanese boy and girl. At first, they sat opposite each other. She seemed sad or moody, head down, picking at her food. He moved to her side and snuggled, head down, joining eating her food. She began to talk very directly - eye contact almost nose to nose - moody. He smiled then, moved back and felt her hair, then pinched a pimple. She kept talking. When I next glanced, she had her feet on the seat of the booth, knees apart, facing him. I couldn't glance for a while, and when I next glanced she was fondling him, foreheads touching. He stood up and so did his erection. They both scooted out to the bathroom. After that I don't know 'cause I had finished my sandwich.

The Age of Leg Jiggling

I taught school before the Age of Leg Jiggling, the now prevalent habit of quick up and down bouncing of one's leg or legs. I first noticed it with boys in the classroom, then girls and eventually adults. I found it hard to concentrate when the entire room was 'jiggling.' During my daily visit to the local cafe when I am writing about my past experiences or visiting with an alum, I've become very aware of the leg jiggling of many of the other customers. There was a table of 12 people, all varieties of ages. During their meeting they all 'jiggled' at different times, sometimes one leg only and sometimes both. Now for my composition idea: If there was a way to attach a note or tone to each person's legs and record it - it might be a wonderful John Cage inspired symphonic piece. Of course, this wouldn't always work as in the case of a young man today, who jiggled both knees continually for one hour except when he blew his nose.

Jewelry

George and I went to Oregon to stay at the Beach House. I wasn't familiar with his habit of watching TV the first day. I didn't want to watch, so I went for a walk by myself to a nearby coffee shop and downtown tourist shops. I did this every day while he watched TV and read. I returned to the house and we took a walk together, with the ocean waves coming in, to get a wonderful clam chowder and walk back before the high waves. The third day instead of going to the town shops, I walked the beach alone - watched a family on vacation jumping the waves, burying each other to their chins in the sand and other activities. For a couple of days I picked up driftwood to make a wonderful necklace.

I was in Greece with Siobhan, who was there to present at an ACTF conference. I just had to hear her give her presentation on 'green' directing. She had some time off, so we went to the beach and wandered on our separate paths. She went into an elegant boutique where a model was wearing a most unusual wooden necklace. She wanted to buy it for me as a memory gift but it was Very Expensive. She had just her credit card and little money. They wouldn't take her card and probably thought no one else was crazy enough to buy it, so they reduced the price and I got the necklace as a wonderful 'memory' gift of the trip.

I was in China and saw this elaborate ivory container with a tiny spoon hooked to the lid. The clerk persuaded me that it was perfect for me so I purchased it. I found out the tiny spoon was for scooping opium out of the container.

Craig was one of my very closest students at Florida Southern who became a top model and movie star. I visited him as often as possible when he worked in NY. On one booking he was sent to Russia where he visited the amber caves and purchased a very large Amber Ring for me. It supposedly has worms in it and keeps you from having cancer.

I went with a tour group to Tetuan, Africa. The guide took us on the usual sightseeing tours which included Persian rugs. We passed a barbershop. My dad was a barber so I was most interested in sneaking back by myself and having a look. On the way back, I passed a shop with jewelry hanging from the ceiling above a wall. There was a necklace made of medium sized wooden balls hung on a string. I went in to price it. The Very friendly clerk was so excited and gave me a price. Next to it was a Much larger wooden ball necklace. I asked the price. He smiled Big and said, "No, No, No, not for sale." I begged him for the price - he bowed and laughed and said, "No, No," then he looked at me, more laughter and said, "Only if you send your oldest daughter."

During school break, I was visiting NYC and staying out on Long Island with Bob's mother. I'd take the train into the city and then a subway to the place or event I wanted to see. I 'dressed' for the play or art gallery or shops I wanted to visit. One late night after getting off the train on Long Island, I walked past a car lot and a drunk jumped out of his car to grab me. He was too drunk to catch me, but after that I stayed in the city with my student, Richard Tatro, who was modeling and acting in Star Wars and lived right off Central Park. When the concert or play was over, I would try to get to their bathroom before it was locked or I would find a telephone booth and cover the windows with a huge cloth, to change into old clothes to walk to his apartment. One night when I was 'poorly' dressed and almost to the apartment, there was an elderly man sitting on the sidewalk with his jewelry display to sell. He called to me - stayed his distance, and showed me this necklace. He said, "I watch you and my jewelry is made as a gift for you." He put it on the sidewalk and walked away.

I was in the pet shop in LaCrosse getting food for my dog. This wildly colored woven item was hanging on the display. I thought it was a necklace. I asked and they said it was a toy for a parrot and I bought it. I had designed a dress to go to NYC for a weekend to meet Siobhan. I had given her a gift of money for turning in my name for an award I got. She was looking for a Real Designer's Purse in all the best stores. I was just looking. A man came up to me all excited, and looking at my necklace said, "That's a Betsey Johnson (famous jewelry designer). I've never seen it on anyone!" I walked away, resisting telling him the real story. Another man passed me at the front door looking surprised and said, "Oh! A Betsey Johnson! Could I take a photo?" I walked back to Siobhan, still looking for a 'Real Designer Purse' and taking pictures and sending them to Shari at home to help her choose. We walked out of Saks Fifth Avenue. I told her the story and then another man walked by and commented, "Could I take a picture? That's beautiful." (The parrot toy necklace, not me.)

I was in Tampa, Florida visiting Paul and Dulcie, and in order to give them a break, George and I drove to the Museum of Salvador Dali. I found this wonderful necklace of a Dali clock and George bought it for me.

Vivian with signature giraffe necklace

Camel Cookies

Now for the camel cookie story. First you must know I planned to die as my Mother before me did - Never Having Baked Cookies.

I chose to make a most difficult rolled out shortbread dough - for color and texture - uh huh.

Well eventually I cut out 35 of these patterns and got most of them into pans without broken necks, etc. The oven didn't work so I rode across town to use my maybe future son-in-law's oven. By this time, I had a backache from nervous strain. The cookies were cooked.

I 'carefully' stacked all the pans and held on while I cautiously headed back to get ready for the party. Some guy came through his stop light. I slammed brakes - heard lots of camels scooting to one end and shouted, "Oh No My Camels!"

I arrived home with some broken necks but still with frosting saddle and harness. I spread them all over the car trunk and started down the Mississippi to LaCrosse with 35 camels. They liked the trip and the Egyptian party LOVED the camels.

Never Again!

Part Five

TRIPS

Venice Twice

The first visit was when Bob and I were hitchhiking through several countries. We were almost the only American students, and were wearing blue jeans. *Correction* - I was wearing *brown* jeans but that's another story in another country.

We walked around the square taking in everything we'd read about. Had coffee at the 'right coffee shop,' and studied the travel guide to decide what to see besides the Venice Biennale which was our priority - a world collection of the best art.

We started over our first bridge to where we were to stay. I looked down and saw a gondolier 'parking his boat' in front of his home. He carefully pulled his oar out of the beautifully carved wood forcola. I said, "That's the best art we'll see. I wonder if we can get one?" Bob inquired with his broken Italian and beautiful Italian book, and skipping lots of details, found out where the forcola were carved and that each family had their own design, and it was arranged for us to go there. We explored several little square neighborhoods and found someone who made fat little church angels. I loved them and the woman selling them. We bought one. After 60 years it still hangs in my bedroom reflected in the mirror. Every morning I smile at it.

So, to stay somewhat on the subject... We followed directions over 'several' bridges to the 'shop' where they were all carved. We tried, but it was really impossible to understand each other, but he gave us the place and time the following morning to go to. So, we went on the next adventure - to find the place we were to stay.

Next morning, with a picture map of where we were to meet someone who could understand us, we went over bridge after bridge and went into an office building. Around a long table sat maybe 15 businessmen in black suits who stood up when we entered and suggested we sit. We had no idea what was going on. After several comments, we slowly discovered the whole Board was there and I think they thought we wanted to buy for all of the U.S. We slowly got across that we only wanted one. I can't write all the details, but we finally ended up with one.

Now the timing to go to Venice was for the art collection at the Venice Biennale. We went there and wandered separately from room to room, taking it all in. I went into one room where there was an elderly man scraping paint off a Giacometti sculpture. WOW. I didn't know whether to turn him in or run and not get involved. I waited and went to the next room. I heard a group singing Happy Birthday. I asked. It was Giacometti scraping his own sculpture! He decided he didn't like the color. His theory was, he created a surface so when it was found thousands of years later, it would be known to be his. Back in the VW and with the top down and baby Santha in her playpen (back of the back seat), we were off to the next country.

A Few Days in Paris

We went to see plays at the Grand Guignol - a famous French theatre known for gruesome plays and blood on stage, etc. The Grand Guignol Theatre looked like a very old converted church. The floorboards creaked, the seats were purple velvet and very saggy, two angels hung from the rafters. The fire curtain that was usually down was canvas - they must have forgotten because I heard years later the theater burned down and never reopened. This one was <u>heavy</u> iron and came down with a mighty *thump*. We saw three short plays - two were comedies (I think) and one was HORROR where a man's face was cut off in full view of the audience, including us in the second row.

Saturday - The hotel and all of Paris filled up with tourists for the big celebration of Bastille Day. We moved to a smaller room - less money. Before breakfast we went to see an original sketch by Matisse brought in by his model. At breakfast we sat next to a very lively group and worked our way into the conversation. One was the leading poet of Sweden; one was an excellent artist now working in Paris. We talked for two hours then took a cab to his home. We had wanted to meet the artist Appel and he knew him, so we went to Appel's studio. We looked at his HUGE painting (oils sometimes over 1" thick), and his entire floor was covered with gallon cans filled with different colored oil paint, ready for his throwing. We met his wife, who is a photographed model.

It was early evening and we decided to be brave and try to get in to see the Folies Bergère - the most spectacular show in Paris. Tickets were sold out, so we bought standing room. There were 500 people in standing room plus 3 balconies full, so you can imagine its size. We got up on some steps and had a very close position. It's the most elaborate show anyone can imagine - 42 tableaus - each more beautiful. Some of the costumes on the girls were at least 12 yards of skirt material - luscious velvets, and some headdresses were 5 feet high. There was a big swimming pool on stage. Gondolas floated by and Much More. I sketched the costumes. After the show, we sat at Our Cave until 2 am listening to bands, firecrackers, street dancers, etc.

Sunday - The next day was walking day. We went to the Arc de Triomphe, walked up 160 steps, and from the top viewed all of Paris - gray stone buildings with very wide tree-lined streets. We walked up and down the Champs de Elyse and looked at all the fashionable shops. We went to Montparnasse and Pigalle (picturesque sections of Paris) and ended up climbing 270 steps to the top of the hill, where the Sacre Coeur Basilica is built and watched the fireworks, then walked slowly home.

Just like every day, Monday we sought out more galleries. We met the sculptor Cesar, a little short man with a huge mustache and big twinkly eyes. Somehow carried on a conversation although he spoke no English.

We wanted to go to the Roland Petit Ballet though our money was tight, but finally decided to try for tickets, which in those days were 50 cents. We got the cheapest ones which were in the balcony (under the light board), so we climbed up many stairs and sat. I couldn't even see the stage, so Bob said, "Stay here, I'll see what I can do," and left. It was TIME to begin, and he was not back. I panicked. Just then the door below opened and he shouted, "Come on, Viv." I never argue, so I gathered our stuff and scooted. We RAN down steps, through doors, and were on the 3rd row on the main floor - almost on the stage. I asked no questions. At the first break, he told me because we were American students (probably the Box Office guy liked Bob), we got The Best Seats.

We had coffee at a very elegant cafe. On our way home we discovered we had enough money for a bottle of perfume. It was closing time. Bob ran six blocks and held the door open. After we had been shown six varieties, we purchased some.

Our last night in Paris, we took a tour of four night clubs. We got home at 3 am, packed, and the next morning went back to England. It was raining. After we got to London, we hitchhiked to Stratford, where we told our stories to the raindrops.

Another Day in Paris

Our Paris ritual is the same. Every morning we had two good oranges in our room, and then went downstairs across the street to 'our' bakery where we pointed to the sweet rolls, two each, and sat on a bench out front, then went to our favorite cafe for morning coffee. We sat and planned our day and watched people. Sometimes we ate at a pretty park, but usually went back to our room where we had French bread, cheese, pate, fruit, and liquid, since we couldn't drink the water.

We had a picnic once in a beautiful park with marionettes for the children. Next to us was a man, not quite all there, playing an involved game with imaginary people. He moved beautifully.

One day we had a good trip though the Louvre Museum. We saw Winged Victory, the Mona Lisa, Egyptian tombs and all the famous painters. It took hours. We also went to art galleries and saw our favorite painters there as well.

We were on our way down a side street to see a sketch done by Matisse and happened upon a Vogue model being photographed in next year's winter coat. It was exciting to watch how she posed.

Boat Adventures in Holland

Bob and I decided to try our luck at hitchhiking all over Europe, or at least several countries. Ray, a fellow scholar at the Shakespeare Institute, asked to go with us (he said he spoke French - fluently), so the three of us set off.

We met at the dock of the English Channel and raised our thumbs. It was Easter and cars were filled with kids & bunnies, etc. No one stopped. A policeman came to us and suggested the two guys hide and leave me out to thumb it 'alone.' The next car was a beautiful car with a beautiful driver, and the back seat filled with dozens of red roses. I put my thumb out.... alone. The two guys came out of hiding and he sped away.

We managed to get to Holland, where we bargained to get a boat. We were shown one that 'slept six,' the man said. Bob mumbled,

"How much does it eat?!" We claimed to be 'sailors' (they had read a book on it). The woman put an American flag on the front and an English one on the back, and handed us a 'little' whistle with instructions to 'toot' when passing another ship, and when we came to a closed bridge (there were at least ten along the river) we should toot 3 times and the bridge operator would appear and open the bridge.

We were off. I was the cook, and the guys took turns playing Captain. A bigger ship went by - they tooted, and we tooted. Bob was dressed in his Harris Tweed suit and smoking a cigar. We passed beautiful homes with flowers, and windows placed so you could see through the house.

As a side note, when the French spoke to us, he said, "They're using the wrong verb!" We did much better with my mime.

Continued....

BOAT ADVENTURES: THE BRIDGE

And now for our first bridge. We were approaching too fast and had NO brakes. A very elderly, slow-moving man appeared out of a little hut on the side of the bridge. I grabbed some coins and made my way out on the deck of the boat. The man looked surprised, nodded, and went back into the hut and appeared with a tin can on a long rope. I tried to reach but couldn't, so the boys jumped up on the boat to help me. We got the coins in the swinging tin and the man started back to the hut to turn the wheel that opened the gate. The boat had NO brakes. Suddenly, the boat scraped against the stones and got stuck - with a small hole on the side. I jumped out and did my usual routine of tying a boat rope around a post.

Skipping MUCH discussion and fear, the boys decided to leave me on the boat and go into town to find help. No one spoke English, word traveled fast, and a group of children appeared on land by the boat. I didn't know what to do, so I decided to teach them English. I got out my lipstick, held it up and said loudly, "LIPSTICK." They giggled and repeated. Out of the corner of my eye, I saw a little boy leave the group, go over to the post where we had 'tied up,' and start to slide the rope up off the post. I screamed, "STOP IT!" Then they all screamed, "Stop It!" The boy did stop, and they left - happy.

The boys returned with No News of help. It grew dark and we sat on the boat with a hole, but not sinking, and discussed over and over what to do. Finally, we saw a light coming toward the boat. It was a young boy with some tools and equipment. He knew NO English, but he FIXED THE HOLE and refused to take money, smiled, and left.

We had many more boat surprises but that's another story!

Seasick on the Ship to Majorca

The weather was fierce! The waves were so unforgiving that the Navy ship didn't leave the shore, but *we* did – on a smaller ship with the purpose of delivering many bulls for the booked bull fight on the island of Majorca, along with a group of young soldiers.

The rocking was SO bad! The worst were the huge waves that played with 'our' ship. The bulls on board were all sick. My friend, who was always reading, told me if we went out on deck in the air, we wouldn't get sick. So, we slowly crawled out and got inside a high wall of wrapped rope.

I went a step further and crawled out on the front of the bow. A soldier saw me and crawled out to me. He reached in his pocket for a hard-boiled egg covered with pocket dirt. He handed it to me, and I think he said – in Spanish – "Eat, and you will be OK."

It didn't work.

The Hunt

It was a wonderful day. We got up early - it was still foggy - and we went with M. Holte, Stratford's professional photographer. Another side note - we had become such good friends through Bob's photographs that although sugar was rationed, he gave us some sugar so we could invite scholars and townspeople over for tea. We went through a number of small villages past Robin Hood's Forest of Arden, the town of Loxley, where we stopped to examine a special gate made for 'ladies with long skirts' years ago, saw wild deer, and finally arrived at the scene of "The Hunt." Holte was hired to take photos. Bob was to assist, and I got to go along. It was amazing! All the riders gathered in the huge courtyard of an inn with these magnificent houses and wearing beautiful riding outfits. Many wore red coats called Riding Pinks, silk top hats, held fancy whips - Real Class.

There were about 75 hounds (we kept calling them dogs). The man in charge called each hound by name. We saw two Lords and a "Lady." She arrived late and was helped onto her saddled horse, and three people arranged her cloaks. She rode side saddle and she shouted "hello" to Britain's world champion jumper - the mayor's son. We watched them being served wine - called stirrup cups - by costumed girls from the Inn. They were all ages; even little kids were in full costume. They discussed and decided on a road to take - in search of a fox. The routine is they send the hounds loose, someone shouts, "Tally Ho," and they're off for a day of hunting across fields, over fences, etc.

We left before they were actually off so Holte could park his car and get ready for the photos. He and Bob discussed the turn of the road, trees and fences, and found "the spot." They carefully calculated wires, branches, fences, and the light. We heard a noise and got ready for some beautiful shots. Someone had arrived at the inn and said, "I say, I hear there's a fox near," and they *went the other way* ... SO ... we got in the car with all the carefully set cameras and went home.

African Adventures

My friend and I decided as long as money lasted, we'd go to Africa. We had been all over Spain. Our greatest problem there - you could be arrested if you kissed in public. We went to Morocco, etc. This story will be about Tetuan.

When we got off the train, we were surrounded by young boys begging us to get a room at their business. We followed one charming boy past a whole new world to where we would stay. He was so anxious to speak English, he offered to take us everywhere tourists NEVER go. His only condition was he had to leave every hour for a short time to worship.

We visited the graveyard, then went to a very expensive wedding. At one point, we were separated. All the women sat leaning against the wall around a large room. No one spoke. I don't remember other details except I wasn't sure I'd ever see my friend again. But this story is about unexpected happenings. He led us up some crooked high stairs to a small room with plastered, cracked walls, once white, that had one window opening - 2 feet by 1 foot. In one corner was a man making tea in a shiny copper container maybe 3 feet tall. Men draped in their local fashion were sitting all around the wall. There was one bench. In front of them were colored water pipes and they were smoking hashish. No one looked up when we entered. I was the only woman. We asked our boy guide, "Isn't this illegal?" He looked surprised and said, "No, we are not allowed alcohol."

He asked us to sit. In minutes, the smell really got to me, so I moved to the tiny window and looked down at all the street below. All the smell was erased by the street sounds and smells. Six men were carrying a dead man (barely draped) on a board high above their heads.

Tribal Jewelry, Grumpy Camels, Arty Bathroom, and Perfume for Prostitutes

A friend visiting Africa went to a tribal ceremony in order to get a necklace for me that "will save you from everything." He knew one was not enough for me, because I liked chunky jewelry multiplied, so he asked for two more necklaces. They insisted one would cure me, so he had to go through two more ceremonies so I'd have three to make the desired effect.

I was in Egypt at the Camel Market. Because of their fierceness, all camels have one leg tied up and the herders carry a knife. They each design their own leather holder for the knife. I fell in love with the design of one and asked for it. Everyone convinced me I couldn't get through customs, so walking away listening to all the grumpy camels, I thought, 'I don't need the knife,' so the boy was flattered I would mean it and gave it to me. Going through customs I got several curious compliments on my necklace.

A friend and I were sauntering down a street in Paris, when I got a call to find a bathroom. We were in front of a major art gallery, so he inquired about painting while I was directed to the back room. It was a huge room. I looked everywhere and could not find a door or sign saying WC, toilette, water closet, or bathroom. I spotted a toilet against one wall, a toilet stool covered with a linen tablecloth and a beautiful place setting, in front of an enormous painting. I removed the table setting and, Don't Ask!

We wanted to have the fun of purchasing perfume in Paris, so chose a perfumery that was beautifully lit with reflections in the mirrored walls. I had been wearing Tabu for years and was known at school for that wonderful perfume. My friend, using a hint of French, asked for Tabu. The irritated clerk said, "Tabu is for prostitutes. We don't sell it."

Costa Rica Stories

I don't know whether I've written the story or not of Rod and I being invited to a very Rich Art Club. He saw all the guests outside so insisted we go back to the hotel – get dressed in our finest, which for me was my black silk dress and he in white linen shorts, blue linen shirt, and bow tie.

We wandered onto the grounds where they were all having cocktails and clever conversation. As usual, he knew the servers of champagne, and as usual I stayed on the side. They always have to come see me when I get bashful or unsure of myself. Rod pointed me out to them and said 'something,' They laughed and brought me a beautiful goblet. I sip and hold it to my side. Well, they kept filling it and it became too much. I told Rod I wanted to walk back to the hotel, so I did while he stayed on. He had hurt his back while picking up his suitcase, but he doesn't get stopped by pain. I walked a short distance back to the hotel and was so glad to get in bed.

Oh, I forgot to tell you, we had decided to join the tourists and eat from the long tables on the beach loaded with the best, and dozens of colored balloons blowing in the breeze. Well, when I awoke, the entire 2 rooms were filled from the tip of my nose to the ceiling with those balloons! He wouldn't tell me how he got them up to the room.

A wonderful memory of Costa Rica was sitting at McDonald's, watching all the fun in the Big Culture Square in front of the National Theatre – vendors, musicians, dancers, and knowing I was to be a guest at that beautiful theatre – an afternoon at the University of Costa Rica with the Theatre Department. Dinner of flaming everything by a charming chef, with a background of a huge swimming pool, glorious clouds drifting across the mountains, and a lighted cross with a mysterious folktale.

ALSO:

Orange, purple wine, gold flowers everywhere
Vendors with 4000 earrings and not able to decide
Tinkling of bells on the goats
4 am Race Cars under our Grand Hotel window

Rum balls on the airline

A lizard in the sink, and a HUGE pig looking like a boar came in to join me in an outdoor toilet

Best of all, I hugged a lovely Indian beggar woman – aged 104

Spice Market

All the food and how it was served

Dress Circle at the Theatre was for singles

My birthday on the plane at New Orleans on our way to Mexico

Musicians on our bus wanted 100 pesos to play Rod's request; he gave them 50 and asked for ½ the song

In my wandering alone, I found a Designers' Bazaar owned by Estevez but nothing to copy

Lots of walking

On another excursion, we went by train to Indian Lanes in the mountains. What an adventure. Before we left, I cleaned all our windows in and out to enjoy the scenery. It was amazing. The Indians all lived in caves – dark – and all very primitive. Children played <u>barefoot</u> on the rocks. The elders sat inside the dark caves – smoking. One man had carved wooden dolls. I had to have one, but which one? They all joined in – toothless laughter – telling me to take all and they wanted to come also. I finally decided – they all clapped and we went back on the tour.

We were walking to our favorite restaurant for our favorite food and people, when we discovered it was Mardi Gras time. The streets were lined with celebrations. Everyone was 'all dressed up.' The floats were packed with sculpture, decorations, music, and people shouting. As they went by, two of the young boys who were from our hotel jumped down and insisted we ride the float together. It was not that easy, and Rod and his sore back still from opening his suitcase, but he doesn't give up. Somehow, they got us with them - Wow! Wow! It seemed to go on for hours. They stopped by a tennis court where Rod played, and we insisted we shouldn't take up their place or time. Well, it wasn't long before the tennis court was filled with the mayor, his wife, and lots of giggly girls. We had no choice. The mayor grabbed me to dance, and his wife did her best with Rod. What an experience!

It was time to go home - pack, pay, say goodbye to everyone, but before we got a taxi, I wanted to go to the cathedral and say goodbye to my little beggar man I kissed earlier. I was wearing my all-white gauze 'outfit' with WIDE LEGS. I caught my foot in the leg going up the steps and sprained my LEFT ANKLE!!! Rituals like taxi, suitcase, and bags of ice got us to the airport.

Rod went behind the counter and 'somehow' changed our ticket to first class, put me in a wheelchair, and two hunky men carried me and the wheelchair up the steps to the plane. My foot was bandaged, and part of it made a sling that they attached to some-thing in the airplane, so I traveled in lots of pain with a leg swinging from the ceiling – home. As usual, I went to a doctor. I can't wait to tell my beautiful girls, but they have their own things to tell me.

Puerto Rico Experience

We decided we should try another experience – ride on a Non-Tourist bus in the Non-Tourist part of town – WOW. We got on the bus – NO seats open – no one even looked at us – all were talking and gesturing. I was dirty and smelled terrible, and the ride into the beautiful countryside seemed different than when we rode through it in a limo coming in. I looked out a dirty window and saw two large women with enormous skirts blowing in the wind and shouting and waving to the driver. He did stop. They got on even though we were already squished together. Under their skirts they had 'hidden' large bags of coffee beans. Why, I don't know. I almost passed out with the strong smell of coffee.

We got off. They got off at the same stop. We followed them and found they were selling the beans. I thought this would be a great gift to bring home, so I bought several bags. Somehow, we got back to our Tourist World and to our Holiday Inn apartment. The coffee smell was So Strong we took the bags to the main office and asked them to keep them in storage. A few days later we packed to leave, picked up our suitcase and coffee bags, and went to the airport. We had a long wait and couldn't stand the coffee smell, so I checked the coffee into a locker. It was almost time to board, and I had forgotten about the beans. So, with a real struggle and some help, the attendant unlocked the locker, and we were off to the gate to check all our luggage. It's unbelievable - the whole plane smelled heavily of coffee, but no one knew who to blame!!

Events Rod Arranged on Our Trips to Puerto Vallarta

I had NO idea where we were going – as usual. A local man who was really sharp picked us up at our hotel and we BOUNCED along to the railroad station. On our way, he told us of prostitutes, coffee, gold jewelry (for the lady), and We Were There!! We walked around our new area of many local on-lookers for 15 minutes while two private cars arrived, and from there loaded onto the railroad was pop, beer, pineapples, bananas, chocolate, sandwiches, plus a Real Character – a Wild Woman Guide.

The antique train was purchased from Germany 60 years before. We boarded for a 10-hour day. The Wild One explained every detail of everything on the way. The train bumped along and often got stuck, and chugged up mountains saying, "I think I can," then sped downhill – past coffee plantations so close we grabbed some. We each had an open window, and because Rod and I sat up front, IT WAS NOISY. We passed bamboo trees and stopped at a banana plantation. We rumbled across creaky iron bridges, through gorgeous meadows, stopped at small villages where kids sold fruit and cookies, added to our lunch on board. We got on a coach of local people, so packed that some stood. All the kids and adults LOVED and FELT my animal necklace. It was a *Fantastic Day.*

A Mazatlán Memory

We had a very large double room beautifully decorated with large green plants – drapes – walls and balcony to sit on looking out at palm trees, an oval shaped swimming pool, and rows of white lounge chairs with a large white towel folded on each. Musicians were playing, a few selling jewelry and clothes, with a backdrop of the ocean rolling in.

Out the side window and across the street was a beautiful building – the art museum. After a leisurely breakfast by the pool, we decided to get a taxi into the main town. We went in and out of boutiques, had drinks and lunch, even danced. A group of musicians was playing in the street in front of one of the shops. They circled around us for us to dance. My bashfulness came over me, even though they all begged, and we ventured on. After lunch the same musicians were playing in a different street and again begged us to dance. Still, I couldn't.

We decided to walk the windy road home past beautiful homes. We had been told two somewhat connecting homes belonged to Elizabeth Taylor and Richard Burton. As we neared those houses, we heard music and much laughter. It came from a huge balcony of Liz Taylor where we were told later, she was throwing a party. We looked up and saw the *same musicians* with the crowd on the huge balcony. They were getting ready to play. They SAW US and from the balcony motioned for us to come up and join them, SO, we can say we were invited to Liz Taylor's party.

Thoughts on Summer Teton Trip

I have never felt such contentment, such peace with myself and the world in my entire life for such a long period of time. This week in the Tetons, I have reached a new me. How silly Rod's social structures seem, and all my conflicts about them. Santha is in David's hands, who is all she needs at the moment – brother, lover, father. Shari and Siobhan are the most perfect traveling companions. This is a first in many ways for me out of our 11 years of camping.

George can be severe, romantic, intelligent, caring, strong – just perfect for Wyoming and the Tetons. At the moment, I can't even imagine having a martini at the country club. Could I be this way always if I was removed from competition, or would I get bored and begin to feel uncreative, unattractive, and into 'it' doesn't matter? I feel no competitiveness, none of the constant nagging I always live with - that I should be doing something other than what I'm doing, always gnawing at me except when I direct in the theatre. But Not Now. No need to direct at all. I can actually think about ME.

At the moment, I am watching another sunset with the full range of Tetons. Voices trail in the distance, pretty butterfly wind surfers breeze by, a gull joins me for a moment. As the sun rises, Shari and I go to the lake, a few steps from our campsite, to sit on our driftwood chairs to read and write. As the sun fades, I no longer feel that great power of the mountains. They look like torn paper against a wild sky. The Tetons are strong but so pretty – feminine.

So many things have led to this peace I've finally reached. Some have been very painful. Sometimes a conversation, sometimes a look, the beauty of just breathing. As Santha said on the phone, "It's about time."

Some Memories – Tetons Postcard

Entering the world of motorcycles put a new perspective on my world. We began to see dotted scooting, zooming everywhere – cycles of all variations. And the look and speech of cycle people. Two HUGE Paul Bunyans with black curly beards passed – twins. Seeing 20,000 cyclists at Sturgis Rendezvous should have been the high point, but no – it was in Deadwood. We watched the most marvelous flirtation between two drunks - dirty, half toothless 20-year-olds while waiting for an ice cream cone.

Having lunch sitting in the spray of Hidden Falls after a four-hour hike. Going back to a great dinner by sunset with tired, aching muscles from a 10-mile mountain hike. Joining for the first time unafraid, the troupe in the clear water of String Lake after a hike. Re-taking a picture of 11 years ago with the girls screaming 'snakes – worms' with sticks. A beautiful afternoon sitting on a chosen boulder reading The Love Hunter, listening to the water splash about me. The excitement of the story built of a man in a duck blind. I'm sorry I didn't read more good books before the floating black lace covered my vision, but I didn't, and now I find I'm looking at everything more than ever.

After the sunset last night, after the camp slideshow, after calling Santha and a Mountain Nudge, George built a marvelous smelling fire and we all lay on the picnic table and watched the sky for shooting stars. After miles and miles of silence, George and I both saw a single sunflower among a field of sage brush. His poem: "Someone's been here and thrown a seed out."

Another gift was a cup of freshly picked huckleberries. A really beautiful surprise was a framed drawing by my favorite Indian artist of a mother and three children. I love it. He called it a nice family portrait. I fell in love with a sculpture by Harry Jackson of Sacajawea in Jackson. It's the first time I wanted to purchase it - the first time I talked 'Art.' Bob did it all before.

The catching of a bear (in a trap) at our campsite was good because of what Barry the ranger's attitude was, he said, "I'm glad for the bear. By catching it, we can take it back to its natural habitat and free it rather than have to kill it." It makes me wonder where my natural habitat is.

The Jackson rodeo was special with Shari and Siobhan, and sitting by a Real Cowboy who knew the rules. We moved into even more majestic mountains - into Canada. A new world.

The twins' Golden Birthday, 18 on the 18th was all flowers and butterflies. We hiked to the top of the Tunnel Mountain, and everyone sang to them. I wrapped presents and trimmed the van in flowers and butterflies to be the most beautiful garden. They were pretty butterflies.

We hiked eight miles up 3000 feet to a private world among real glaciers thousands of years old to wait for avalanches – we saw three. Fun little moments like the first night out. Siobhan was in charge of music (new to this trip). In order to stay awake she had to keep singing – she got a sore throat. When we got *the* flat tire and went to get air, the machine made good modern music, so Shari and Siobhan began to dance to it.

And much more....

Somewhere among the wild waterfalls, free animals, and us I got this quote:

"Echoes of timeless struggle assault our senses."

Postcard

"Roots make good stepping stones."

After a week of breathing in the beauty of the Tetons, and hours of hiking through it all with our special rituals of the past eight trips - our new ones added - we are heading for dinner at Trolley Square, Salt Lake City, then to where I had my first teaching job ever, when I married, then on to Bogue, Kansas, my hometown. We will then have a big birthday party for Shari in our back yard, then home for the wedding and we start again!

How I Met Don

I was at a Theatre Conference in San Francisco. It had ended. I went back to the hotel to pack wondering what to do – hours before my plane.

I decided to go a few blocks to a café I found. I walked two blocks (without my suitcase) and stopped at a Red Street Light. A man came up and waited at the same light. We both waited and waited (it was broken) and I said something. A guy was carrying a huge painting out of an art gallery. We both turned.

He said, "What do you think?" I said, "A 'B'." We started talking art and he asked if he could buy me a cup of coffee. We went to my favorite café and talked and talked.

He was recovering from a Divorce and I was recovering from Something. He talked Architecture and asked if I had visited the Modern Museum. I was done with meetings SO with time to spare we went to the museum – he knew the architect, etc.

When it was time to go, I asked him how to get back to my hotel for my bag. He said he'd take me. We were both staying at the same hotel.

He invited me and (insisted) the family come visit him in Vancouver. Thus began a friendship that lasted a lifetime.

Don's House in Vancouver

We turn into the driveway of Don's self-designed world. White plastic sculpture in trees. The steps of round shaped colors of marble, a cedar wall not seen before, the new neighbors moved in, blackberries full and plump and ready. The forgotten sculpture sensuously leading me on past cedar walls with new art hung up, the French postcards - a memory of a past trip framed to perfection with gray and rust mats perfectly spaced, the Barcelona poster - another memory of our times framed. Past closed doors of his office and open kitchen, with new everything carefully chosen, down steps across black and white marked floors. Greek carpet to lower deck to a goblet of wine from a chosen blue bottle and nachos in a blue shell shaped dish. On one side, a black leather sofa, and I saw a gift of mine on the glass top sculptured coffee table - various collections of my past gifts placed among the keepsake memories from many exotic places. The office door opened where he had been checking out details for a Baja Temple in Israel (he was the architect).

I did dishes while looking out at the sailboats and a ship on its way to Alaska to vacation, then up to the library to enjoy shelves of adventure and art, combined with his squeaky desk chair and phone calls to Haiti about artist Chadwick, and David's (his son) graduation in architect Erickson's court house. More photos on the upper, open hallway purchased in London and South America, a framed label of wine purchased in Vernazza, and a postcard of his parents' wedding in their Wales home. All this with the feel of a gossamer, soft blue scarf with shell designs wrapped about me.

I was so aware of me in these sensuous surroundings, bare feet on tight textured Greek carpet - wine gummy candies in my mouth - the sound of pen on paper, kids in boat below, occasional flying birds above the skylight, car driving up the gravel driveway, perhaps Colin for his moment of flirting. The door to the blue bath slightly ajar, door to cedar sauna - with huge wooden bucket and ladle, oversized bath towels in rust, blue, and brown - South American woven rug in burnt orange on the floor.

We had lunch in the dining area with last night's spinach triangle in phyllo with lemon sauce on Haiti blue and beige plates. This area was filled with his glass table set over a black foundation, and six Eames chairs covered with black and gray mats I had sent, with bronze candle holders. A matte black crumb brush and holder we found in San Diego were on a window shelf. I was seated looking at the sailboats below. When it was time to go, I passed dishes through the kitchen window - "We have chocolate to eat later."

I went back to the wine gummies and the luxurious feel of the Eames chair that switched in all directions so that I might see the first view of the master bedroom, with the triple bed covered in huge brown and blue pillows and the wall with framed pictures of Haiti. "In 30 minutes I'll be done, and we'll go downtown." I changed into pants and a top created from a sheet. "Wowie," says Don.

San Francisco Escapade

While on quarter sabbatical, I 'did' the West Coast. I stayed with Lois in Phoenix. We went to a nightclub and the entertainment was a guy who once played with Bernadot's band. Of the many adventures staying with Jerry Cushion and wife (years ago we did Community Theatre with him in Salina, Kansas). I had arranged to stay with Mat Streater (another story) to attend class at ACT, but the Big Deal was to see the play Fool for Love at Magic Theatre. When I arrived in San Francisco, I was held back from all the other passengers to examine my suitcase. It turned out the sniffing dog didn't like my Tabu perfume.

I had problems taking buses and finding Mat's apartment so after walking blocks, I hid/left my suitcase in a closed newsstand and hoped. Mat and I went back, and it was still there! I found details on the bus to Magic Theater – a long bus ride from Mat's. The play was FIERCE. I had written I was on sabbatical, so had a free ticket in the FRONT ROW and next to the playwright.

When the play was over, I stayed and talked and then went to catch the bus. It didn't come and it didn't come, so I started walking – a dark night. As I got closer to the main center of San Francisco and Mat's apartment, all doorways were filled with prostitutes – some women, some men, and some changing their mind and wildly dressed. Several stepped out of hiding and asked who I was and why I was walking in that neighborhood. A Very Tall Male dressed as a Woman offered to walk with me out of that neighborhood. Mat was shocked and happy to see me. A week later when Don came to meet me, I asked to be taken back to that section to see my Friend and others to thank them. Don was surprised to watch our little farewell party.

Con Man on the Bus

The bus ride from Portland to Seattle was enhanced by lessons in communication involved in the con world. All the info came from the seat behind me. A big, burly guy who was down and out on his folks' farm, raising a cat with 6 or 7 toes for selling, drinking quarts of milk. With each encounter his voice and his vocabulary changed - something only a con man would learn - never mentioned in speech courses.

A young Chinese couple looking for an apartment got an efficient run down of prices and availability in each section of Seattle, a young guy who wanted to go back to college got an intellectual report on colleges, and an ex-hippy sat beside him - language change to where to get drugs, fake driver's license and which were the best copies. He got off to meet his cat buyer. I got off to call Mario. The bus broke down for one hour - interesting passengers:

Girl with two front teeth out with her cute black child. She was a truck driver but couldn't solve the problem; two gorgeous black girls in the latest black fashion, low hip trousers and many studs and jewels, one had all gold front teeth; a Big Black Guy in the Best of Black Fashion - most expensive shoes, trousers low in crotch and buckling at the ankle, and HUGE top with E LEWIS in big letters and lots of tags I didn't understand - all BIG and Most Classy, and when we went into a bar to get warm, the owner almost passed out at seeing this Big Star Wrestler...or boxer?

Three Magical Journeys

The lost visa was replaced after five hours of phone calls to recorded voices. The advantage of living in Winona; both the Post Office and UPS held the mail and phoned me when the new visa arrived and told me how to get in the back door. I flew to New Orleans. Because of tight connections, George had a cart waiting for me to transfer. Got to Orleans - was called "Honey" eight times in the process of looking for my lost bag. It had gone to Memphis! What was important was that it had in it the only "gimmick" I had for my speech at the National Convention - my rag doll.

Thanks to Sio going there first and phoning info. I found the shuttle to the hotel - another five "honeys." She found out my age. Amazed I was traveling alone. Oh Honey! Just as I was arriving at the hotel - out came Huge Black Men swaggering in white suits, shoes, shirts, ties, and lavender hats - The Football Team from KC.

Everyone along the way gave me the message that Sio had

arranged the room adjoining hers with the door between - l was to go to my room and then go to another room to watch her rehearse what was to be presented at 8 pm. It was 6 pm. I opened the door - WOW - queen bed all done in dark brown with beige zig zag stripes. I found her. It was wonderful. No one knew me or what I do. She said, "Oh, there's my mom," and introduced me. It was wonderful to be her mom. I watched all their reactions to her directions. Five groups of teachers, actors, and dancers created a show all about the New Orleans disaster. As it got closer to 8:00 it was Panicville. Fun to see her in charge. The five shows were good. I'll tell you about the last one later if you can stand to listen. I was so amazed she managed to dance (the water coming in).

The conference program had all the wrong names. I was depressed and didn't want to show up for the speech. Between all her meetings, she contacted the President (conference). I was treated regally, hugged, and invited to parties. I felt too bashful to show up. Saturday morning at 7:30 am the suitcase arrived, thanks to Sio checking and pushing. It was delivered to her room - the rag doll was there. Now I HAD to go!

I found the room. The audience poured in - packed - even sitting on the floor. Sio arrived. On stage was the ATHE President, a man called Jewell who didn't believe in Method/Laban, etc. A stiff woman from Stanford - in charge of the PhDs (I had to follow her), and the next president who had lots of handouts. We each had a short time for intros and then 25-minutes each. WOW. Anyway, I got lots of reactions from my "simple" statements and a standing ovation. It Was Over.

We got in the lobby - party bands, cheerleaders, TV mascots, etc. I sat, felt something on my shoulder. It was two mascots on both sides hugging me. Someone ran for a camera.

Sio and I walked Bourbon St. It was so steamy hot we went in every shop and five jazz bars (she put in her 'not' hearing aids). We missed the strip bars. She had made reservations at an elegant restaurant for early dinner. I had wonderful, highly seasoned oysters. Now everyone was out walking, shouting, dancing - music, beads, and lights. We played till we were exhausted. She had an early meeting Sunday morning.

We took a four-hour tour of New Orleans with a great guide. He was tuned into each movie being made and each star. We saw a sign saying, DO NOT MOVE - for a movie set, a refrigerator on a roof, school bus through a house. Oh, the politics for millions of destroyed homes. A new wall was built but the same height as the last one - a few new houses built in the same place. More Problems.

We took the shuttle to the airport. There were many more people than the van could hold, so again she stepped forward and used my connecting time and heart problems and INSISTED, so I got the front seat. She got the heavy luggage handled and we were off - just in time! It was a pain to carry a huge straw hat - for the beach, etc. At Minneapolis she contacted a cart. She went ahead and said I had four minutes to connect to Vancouver. What a woman she's grown into. So easy to be with and so caring.

Part II

I arrived early in Vancouver - got through customs easily even with my foot-long hat pin. Got so many compliments on my animal necklace, rings, and hat (what I hide behind).

Don was waiting. I had forgotten how amazing the airport design is. WOW! I forgot how fast Don speaks, how much info he knows about each building, how magic Vancouver is at night. We arrived at his super designed home, boats in the water below, stories of neighbors' billion $ mansions and people I knew, and plans made and wanting to stay longer. Whee! It all started - a new adventure. So different, the energy! The Artistic Beauty! I glanced over at his display of art books, photos, and gifts I've given him. There was something - a perfect shape, color, texture to make a ring. I picked it up - a bite of bread left out. Into my room to unpack - given beautiful towels. Really clean house ready for parties. Lots of phone calls - welcoming me.

The daily routine was to sleep late, breakfast on the deck watching the boats below - the ocean liner - the School of Sailing. Don's three grandchildren, ages nine and ten, had been enrolled in classes - then went out alone (on each boat) or looking at his photos of world travels and trying to tell me stories - without success - interrupted. Exotic foods presented, then change clothes to drive downtown for the daily coffee routine. Coffee shop was in a new village with expensive shops. Pure snobbery. They advertise, 'Why Pay Less?'

We arrived, and there sat the very handsome friend of Don's, Wolf, his shaded white hair and suntan shining in the sun. We joined him, and the clever conversation began. Wolf is worldly, fun and we covered every topic. Other regulars joined - Randy and a Pakistani named Fourd came up to me and sang Sinatra songs competing with Michael Bublé. We spent hours there most days. A perfect model walked by daily in the most perfect clothes who Wolf called Broomstick and other most interesting viewing.

First Party

Other activities - celebrating the 11th year of Don's heart transplant. Nancy, my favorite, arrived with her Bag of Gin. She and Wolf argued about how to make the corn and potatoes. I cut LOTS for Greek salad. We were busy. Guests arrived, brought dishes and bottles. Each were very different types, and conversation zoomed. A man who cycled all over the world; a retired doctor who skis from a helicopter and artist wife; a woman who lived on and ran a boat for 20 years, etc. They left at 2 am.

Second day there - Don dropped me off at the AETA conference. We toured Indian fabric shops, ate at a most-most restaurant at the waterfront crowded with boats. I had goat cheese soufflé and mussels displayed artistically, then off to the fireworks - competition between countries.

The news was turned on just 1/2 hour and heard about the bridge disaster.

Toured the Art Museum and had a drink on the roof with guests - piano and bass - and Don's info on all new buildings - What a city!!

Time to catch the bus (phase 3 of trip). Heavy, heavy suitcase - so grateful for people who helped. I was to have a three-hour layover in Seattle and planned to get a cab to Ivor's and watch them throw fish, etc. but we were two hours late so on to the bus.

Portland - so nice to see George come slowly forward. We drove all over Portland then to his home. Plans changed because Dean (George's brother) had friends at the Beach House, so we stayed with his mother for three days. She endlessly serves her males, and she had a great time or appreciated me - because she never really talks to women, and my age (a secret) helped her understand her stories of "those days." Dean graced us twice with his presence. He's frantic, very quick, intelligent, and argumentative, looks like Einstein with his wild hair – most difficult to be with – with the family. He and George tried to do a bathroom fixture Sue wanted – it was so frantic. George said nothing and I had to go for a walk.

When we went to Dean's magazine-worthy designed office for our email, and he was with me alone, he could really pour on the charm - he was quite different. He does research for companies - just got a 5 million, five-year job. He does research for the state on who wears seatbelts (he got six tickets this year for not wearing one).

Are you still reading??? It gets better. I chose not to go to a Greek family dinner event even though Sue was disappointed - she wanted me included.

I was dropped off at Starbucks on 23rd Street for three hours. The street is lined with boutiques and outdoor musicians, neat people. I walked both sides taking in everything. I found a pretty, wooden bench and "sat a spell," as my mother would say. A once elegant man, 70's, now a street alcoholic came up and asked if he could sit. I said yes but didn't know how long I'd be there. He had a British accent, born in Germany. As he sipped his hidden beer, we had the best conversation. I asked questions. He talked in detail about fashion, architecture, music (he played the cello) - comparing cities, countries, how many times he had been in jails and where - how he loved the beauty of the world. He had quit drinking 5 times. He was (and still is) in love with a beautiful woman and was sober, but a 'friend' offered him a drink and he was stuck. He couldn't recover. His friend married the woman. He had tears at this point. I'll never forget him - a highlight of the trip. I had to meet George. As I walked away toward Starbucks, I looked back and he was asleep lying on the bench. As he had said – "probably in jail tonight."

I wanted to back up and tell you about our dinner at Disneyland. A friend of Don's joined us and suggested we should come to his "Disneyland house" for dinner. Another friend who is an excellent cook (and appears at the coffee house round up) said, "Let's make it tonight before Viv leaves." Wolf, chef, a woman who belongs to their singles club (made up of 75 members who like to travel, etc. but don't want to get married again). Don and I arrived at this home created by his daughter.

The daughter, probably in her 30's, is a stunt woman in many top movies. They took the original house and added her requests making it into a castle with a drawbridge, flaming lights, a living room, dining room, and kitchen the size of a huge house with amazing furniture and a round deck overlooking the city lights. The sofa was 12 ft. covered in soft green leather in front of a wall of fireplace and movie screen and a curved counter in the kitchen side. Well, we arrived, crossed the drawbridge and WOW - flaming lights, a small scooter, and drinks on the deck while the food was cooking. Four large, whole salmon with different sauces displayed and lots of fun conversation. After dinner a House Tour.

A big closet with all of the daughter's stunt costumes. Her hand carved four-poster bed was the size of my whole bedroom. Each room had a TV screen the size of a door. There were Jacuzzis in each room, with beautiful sound piped in. Father had a complete part of the house by himself – fully furnished.

Now to the lower level. I didn't know what the chef was saying when he asked me to join him in the jacuzzi earlier. Dessert and drinks were served at the bar (totally equipped) by our muscle-man chef. There was a wall of CDs and by pushing a button it opened to a cave-like Elizabethan Room with carved table, 12 high back chairs, fireplace, and 2 ft. tall candle holders. On to Father's work room and a neat line up of small scooters to the real bikes, 8 I think. Oh, I forgot to tell you - one way to get from upstairs to downstairs was a playground tunnel.

On to the Coast

After shopping for a week's supply and a winding drive through all the trees, greenery, flowers...we arrived. A beautiful brown house with white trim. (Like home in Kansas but how different!) I had never ever seen a house like this growing up. I checked out what had changed. What a dream, stay here for a week with just George (and his cell) and watch the ocean roll in.

Our routine is creating dinner, bed at midnight, and sleeping until 10. George makes his business phone calls, I write and play and walk down to my favorite coffee shop to meet and watch people, then go by all the shops. George's reaction is to sleep, TV, read Lewis and Clark; 5 p.m. adventure ride/tour and take in the Oregon Coast world.

We met Rod Searle. (He was Speaker of the House in the Legislature, then Education Board etc.) He has been our friend since George used to fly the legislators. I had a salad of 9 ingredients (including shrimp and crab) and feta dressing presented in a large bowl piled 4" high. Always needs a take-home box.

We drove north and toured the seaside where the National Volleyball Tournament was, we didn't watch. And sea lions that have a terrible voice then north to Astoria. George re-lived his road paving days with his dad. The regatta was on with lots of ships. A huge woman holding a fish about 38" long got angry at her smaller husband and hit him with the fish!

I reread A Gift from the Sea by Anne Lindbergh. It has a different feeling now that I'm grown up. The beach is filled with sail surfers. Kites in the sky and they're jumping the waves.

My walk about the shops brought me to a new boutique

(playing Michael Bublé's CDs). It's a different meaning since Santha and I went to his live concert, and I became a groupie.

Oh, we used up Dean's expensive toilet paper, so we went shopping! We found Ultra Quilted (16 in a package) and read the sign wrong. It said Buy 2 (this was covered) and get one free. Their mistake so we came home with 36 rolls - our legacy.

Today I wore my black straw hat - for sun protection walking downtown - picking and eating blackberries and blueberries from the bushes. A woman in a limo stopped and said, "You're beautiful, you made my day." A little boy, followed by his mother carrying a baby, looked up and said, "Mom, check this out."

Sitting in the coffee house watching scenes better than any movie and writing notes (a play maybe). The owner was talking to a very clever man. She called me over and introduced me as a college professor. He leaned on the counter and said, "Wow, is that what they look like these days!?!"

A father and his kids sang 'You are My Sunshine.' I haven't heard that song since Kansas. Next scene - in my script. A father playing with his son - in German. The boy traded German and English for some time, then the boy said something in German and the father laughed so loud and hard he almost fell off his chair - not in English or German.

Last night George came in, took my hand, and led me into the dark living room and we silently looked up at thousands of stars and the Big Dipper.

Another coffee house scene - easily the sexiest - more than any movies:

A quick moving girl, 20ish, reminded me of Santha earlier. Guy is tall, baggy clothes, good-looking, foreign, very blue eyes. She sat reading the paper. He stood next to her looking so loving, so sexy. He moved closer - she read. He began to massage her back and say little things to her - beautiful voice. She didn't respond. His hands moving on her were beautiful. She ignored him. (I wanted him to move to my back.) They left the cafe. Next day they came in - she's sporty, well dressed, he's the same. He gets a magazine to read, she looks at him and begins hugging him. She had bruises on her face and neck.

We went to the sand sculpture contest. We missed the Blue Angels. I'm beginning to panic. We have one more day before we leave our wonderland and go back to Portland and HOME. I'm glad I have Winona to go back to.

Trip with WSU Choir to Italy

I traveled with the WSU choir to Rome, Venice, Florence, Sienna and ended at the International Music Festival at Innsbruck. I took a side trip with some friends in a rented car to Oberammergau. The choir sang beautifully in every major cathedral. My arms were waded with cameras each time to take photos of the students singing. Some of the favorite highlights were:

The choir in the catacombs - St. Peter's toes are gone from people touching and kissing them since I was there 37 years ago.

The cats are gone from the Coliseum. Our dramatic guide said they were in our last evening's soup. Thank God the pigeons - the great-grandchildren of the pigeons that flew around Santha (my oldest daughter) when crawling in St. Mark's Square - were still there.

Next to my favorite fountain in Rome was a self-appointed, whiskered guard who brought his own chair and had a string tied to his finger, which was attached to a bottle of wine cooling in the fountain.

After climbing the mountain at Innsbruck, I made an angel in the snow - didn't cause an avalanche and designed what I would create out of all the gorgeous mountain patterns if they were silk.

In Rome, Florence, Sienna, and Venice we had LOTS of pasta - different shapes.

I crawled up one of the huge crosses - a stage prop used for the passion play at Oberammergau - I got to see and feel all the costumes and get answers to all my many questions about the "business" of the play with a young, handsome actor who is coming to visit next year.

Hoping to find a perfect picture for next year's Christmas card, I grabbed at the foot of David (the one not damaged by a deranged tourist years ago) while Bill Laehn attempted to photograph David and I - alone, some task!

The most exciting event happened in the bathroom of my private hotel room. The room was large with a sink the size of a baby changing table, and a mirror that slanted toward the floor. I had to get on my knees in order to make up my face. On the towel rack was one large waffle-like tablecloth and in another, two beautifully pressed linen towels. The huge floor was tiled. The shower stood open without a curtain or door, inviting me to refresh myself. I entered the space. There was NO attached shower head above but a similar device dangling down from a metal flex cord attached to something. I picked up the "device," turned on the water, and this monster got loose from my grip and went crazy flinging itself all over the bathroom ceiling, walls, and floor with me dodging the dancing water. I spent a long time on my knees with the tablecloth soaking up the running water.

I found a tiny cafe - Le Cafe - near the hotel in Innsbruck -

No tourists. The walls - murals beautifully painted, the bathroom mirrored, and sparkly pink toilet paper. Just five small, high tables on one side with a cushioned bench all along the wall blended in with the murals in back. I ordered a rum ball and espresso. It came beautifully served in dark green china with a pretty wrapped chocolate on the side. The now blonde Brazilian waitress greeted me with a wide-open, beautiful smile that never stopped. This buxom beauty was dressed in jeans slit all the way up the side. A friend had crocheted the filler plus a scant top in bright red yarn. She glowed! The owner arrived - an "all Italian" hairdresser who won 4th in a world competition of hair styling and had huge trophies to prove it. His 80+ father arrived and stood by one of the little tables and sang opera to me. I grabbed the glasses. It shook the place. They found CDs of people they thought I liked from the U.S. then the "waitress" put on Brazilian music and danced between the tables. The place was jumping with just us. After many kisses on each cheek, I returned to the tour.

On one long stretch of plane ride, my seating partner was a young girl with a severe case of compulsive beautifying of herself. She arrived with 3 cases of cosmetic products. She proceeded to use all of them step-by-step on her face - each eyelash was stoked and then she would cleanse it all off and start again - all this looking through a tiny broken hand-held mirror leaning against the airplane window. All this I found interesting until she opened the case with the nail polish, and did steps 1, 2, 3, and 4 in that enclosed plane. My head! I became very high and left to walk the aisles. When I returned, she was starting on step 1 again? I took a deep breath and said, "Please don't, it makes me ill." She said in English, "OK," put it away and went back to the face routine.

The Tour was more than I could hope for. The choir singing

in each major cathedral was most moving and added to the religious atmosphere. The university students were fun to travel with and share their excitement.

I had only one real disappointment. On my trips, I look forward to the changing shapes of the haystacks. I've always thought they would make a good calendar of my trips. This time they stayed the same in each country, plus many were wrapped with that vein blue/white plastic that looks like innards.

Changes I noticed since my last trip to Rome, Venice, Florence - years ago:

~Italian men weren't pinching women, but we weren't on public transportation.

~The beautiful theatre in Venice, where I was once a guest, burned down.

~Peggy Guggenheim's home, where I spent many hours and her gondoliers let Santha (in her pram) play with the Calder mobiles - is now a museum and she's buried in the yard. ~In Florence, I once had a mold made of my hands, which stayed at the shop. When living in England at the time, I sent scraps of fabric to match leather gloves they created. Gone is such luxury. ~There were no trim/fabric shops in Innsbruck. I once purchased (yards) of fun trim I used on the girls' clothing for years. ~I did find the restaurant still existed - the spot where Julius Caesar was stabbed (the forum was closed that day). I dined there and an elegant waiter asked in broken English if he might remove the head from my fish.

WSU to Athens, Greece

I went to Athens, Greece with my daughter, Siobhan Bremer, to an international conference on the visual and performing arts (papers read by participants from 19 countries). Siobhan presented on Environmental Theatre using PowerPoint to demonstrate 'green' theatre and a theatrical production she directed at Morris University of MN. The play was written by a WSU alum, Forrest Musselman.

After 20 hours of travel, we arrived at the hotel. Stunned by the beauty and elegance of the lobby in black and beige, and unsure yet how far our euros would go, we took our own bags up to our assigned rooms with our "room" cards (that I can never make work until 3 tries to get a green light).

Oh dear, the rooms are opposite the elevators. Sio had emailed three weeks earlier that she had a sleeping problem and could not be by an elevator. She told me, "Don't do a thing," and went downstairs to complain. She returned with two new door cards, and we went up to 504 and 505. I rolled in my overloaded bag of indecisions of what to wear, and a HEAVY carry on bag full of all the things that might be lost by the airlines. I switched on the light - no result. I tried again. No result. I had to go to the bathroom, and it was dark so I tried the switch again. No result. I heard a noise in the hall, so I opened the door and found a "housekeeper." She smiled and showed me to slide my card key in a wall slot. I thanked her and she left. I slid it in and out - the lights went on. I moved my two heavies out of the hallway and started for the bathroom. The lights went out. By this time, I was desperate. I felt my way through the heavy plexiglass (well heavy something) door into a dark bathroom. I found the stool, sat down, and a swinging metal thing hit my left elbow - my crazy bone. I later found out it was a metal shield with toilet paper inside attached to 2 seven-foot-long beaded ropes swinging from the ceiling. The heavy plexiglass door swung forward on its own and hit my arthritic right knee. I managed to remove the toilet paper from the trapeze, and it flew out and landed in the toilet bowl. I had kicked over another metal container on the right side of the stool which contained a bowl cleaner brush. I used it to dig the big roll of soaked paper out of the bowl. I got it out by chasing it around the bowl and stepped back on a pedal that opened a tiny metal container. Trying to get out of the situation, I stepped back several times on the pedal. Between the rolling metal brush holder, the swinging trapeze that kept hitting the trick door and the pedal opening and closing the other metal container, I was creating music John Cage would be proud of.

Somehow, I got the small metal lid open long enough to put the soaked toilet paper in it. I had put down my door card somewhere in the dark.

I heard another sound in the hall. It could have been Siobhan, but by this time I had no idea I was in Greece or with her. I opened the hall door and found another housekeeper and begged (in mime) for help with the lights. Again, she put my card in the wall holder and the lights went on. She smiled, I smiled, and she left the 'Do Not Disturb' card on the door. It was a beautiful room with heavy drapes, a HUGE bed, a TV, a fridge, a safe, white sofa, and only two pillows, not the 5 different sizes and thickness choices I had staying at Paul and Dulcie's.

I started to unpack and decided to check out the mysterious bathroom and see what damage I had done. And all the lights went out. Back to find the housekeeper. Once again, she explained (mimed) how to put the card in the wall slot. I argued (in mime) and she mimed that I must leave it there for the lights to stay on. P.S. I hope I remember to take it out with me when I leave the room so I can get back in.

It was absolutely necessary to take a shower, so I went into the lightly lit bathroom. I stepped into the tub, the bottom was slanted and slippery. I couldn't stand up and I was too stiff to sit on the ledge. I couldn't depend on the half tub-length plexiglass door to hold me steady, so I put on the glamorous white robe and looked for the housekeeper. She had other things to do besides wait on me, so I boldly tried to call housekeeping. I'm afraid of all phones. A voice said he'd be right up, and he was. He explained in the usual Greek flirtatious, charming manner they had no mat. So, I put a towel in the bottom of the slippery tub. He smiled, waved, and left me.

There was a contraption in the tub wall that looked like the panel for a spaceship. It was oval-shaped, HUGE, with no instructions except on one knob. I could barely turn it. Well, I turned and turned with great difficulty, and nothing happened until all of a sudden, the "fill the tub" came on, and I stood firmly on my towel. I didn't give up. I combined all sorts of turns and suddenly tiny bullet streams of water attacked me from all the spigots. The water sprayed against the half plexiglass swinging door and the tub, and sprayed the entire bathroom.

I escaped once I got the water turned off. I grabbed a huge towel to wipe up the mirror, sink stand and walls, and crawled around to wipe up the slippery tile floor, and found under the sink a huge, heavy set of barbells in a glass case.

Trips to Egypt

On this particular trip I was at the market in Cairo and drifting from shop to shop, and wandered into one where our leader was buying. I found a ring in a dirty box – I had to have it – my friend said, "Put it back and leave and I'll handle it." He bargained and finally (I was waiting outside) he got it for _? I was wearing it and an 'authority' saw it on my hand and said it was a Royal ring to be used to stamp official letters sealed in wax. I must not take it out of the country – So, I hid it.

On another trip to Egypt, my roommate went with her group to join their table at our first meal. As usual, I was too bashful and didn't want to go to the dining room. When I did go, all tables were filled except one where there were three men. They all stared, and I joined. Conversation was Great! There was an elderly gentleman (Les Brady) from a mansion with lots of servants in North Africa. His wife had died, and he had gone into a travel shop and said, "Find me a trip." It turned out to be the one I was on. We became great friends and while everyone went back to their rooms to write, Les took me out for dinner, belly dancing before he'd let me eat or drink. He ordered and tested *everything* before he'd let me eat or drink. He asked me to bring my girls over, and if he had to be gone – he had nurses to help. I should have done it but got so busy. We wrote. He had a birthday party with all his political friends' pictures on a long fence, and mine. When he died, I got a wonderful letter from his daughter.

Other memories were a ride on a camel. They are fierce animals – had two attendants each to hold while I was lifted up. I don't know what happened, but my guard dropped the rope, and the camel went OFF. I thought I would be seeing sand the rest of my life, but they finally got it under control.

I went on a tour to see where all the camels lived. They all had one leg tied up and heavily fenced in. I went to a shop across the street. The usual things were for sale. I looked on the wall and there was a necklace made of yellow balls and a silver chain. I wanted to buy it and he said OK. There was another one with all huge balls (like Louise Nevelson would wear). I Really Wanted it, but he said, "Not for sale – unless you send me your beautiful daughter!"

All the camel guards had knives in a case – they each had designed a 'special' case for it in case a camel got bad. I tried to buy one. The young boy said No – then he realized I only wanted the *case* for a necklace - "OK." He smiled and gave it to me.

Siobhan and I went on a Caribbean Cruise over Spring Break. We cruised - and ate and ate by night and islanded till 6 by day, and ended in Old San Juan and the Barbados Rum factory with heavy molasses smell and lots of samples.

Weekend Local Travel, October 1996

I don't deserve two Great weekends in a row, do I? Last weekend was Gorgeous, so I dressed for the occasion, got out my VW convertible and took off - top down - up the MN side of the Mississippi, my dog Lake by my side. We drove up stretches of highway that hugged the side of the bluffs, winding precariously close to the Mississippi. Sailboats dotted the water; wildflowers were everywhere shouting colors - one of our president's wives passed a law that x amount of $ must be spent on roadside flowers, and we got our share! I quietly thanked her.

I stopped in a tiny town and talked to a woodcarver of carousels and wild birds. We went for a fun beer in a local tavern with local talk I like. I stopped and walked the pier at Lake City. A crowd had gathered to see the largest 'ship' I've ever seen anchored. I was surrounded by lots of boat talk and weathered faces. No offer for a ride though. I ended up at Red Wing at the Fall Craft Show at the St. James Hotel.

Because the bluffs caused 'brrr' and shadows on the open convertible, I crossed over to the Wisconsin side. Ahhh, it was sunny and blazing with colors. I walked out to the edge of the public pier and thought about putting my feet in Lake Pepin, but sat on the car and looked at the misty stillness of the day and thought of good memories.

I could have been in Greece, Majorca, oh - lots of places. An old Soo Line train blew through. I stopped and lingered in little art galleries where I looked at much too delicate paintings and jewelry. I stopped at The Creamery for chunks of cheese and a two-scoop, homemade ice cream cone.

Another town offered the most delicious hot fudge sundae I've ever had, and an antique shop had Antigua coffee. I recalled seeing Helen standing in that shop, hands clasped and smiling at the doll - a nice memory. I buzzed up and up a winding road to the park overlooking miles of the Mississippi with tiny boats and barges. Lake ran free. I sat on the edge of a boulder and remembered. I used to take the girls up there often on Sunday to play all their games. We (Lake and I) continued winding around looking at people's yards and homes and the whole big color splash and the birds making formation ready to go south. The huge fluffy clouds could mean snow comes soon to some.

The next little town had a friend who creates Folk Art and is becoming nationally known and his shop was OPEN, so Lake stayed in the convertible, and I went in to see all his new work.

Across the street and down a bit, I stopped to leave a note on the screen porch door of my photographer friend's home. She is a large mannish woman, part Indian, drives a pick-up truck, teaches at Winona State, returned from photographing all over Europe for magazines. She is never home - now in DC - one of the guards for the last showing of the AIDS Quilt. All the leafers and bikers were heading north to return home, so Lake and I scooted back to meet George.

Gay Wedding

Kathy at the Acoustic said, "Can't you do anything ordinary?" So...

I went to NY City and stayed with Kim Schultz to attend my first Gay Wedding. Ex-students from years ago. The Wedding was Glorious and Such Fun. We walked a mile through huge rocks, fall leaves, sculpture, huge water bubbles, lots of stops past the Huge Alice in Wonderland sculpture in Central Park.

The wedding itself was about 30 people in a circle around the 2 guys in front of a favorite sculpture, and the city in the background. When the ceremony was over - beautiful readings, a violin player - Giggles a Great Wind. It got dark and we all ran for the Metropolitan Museum. I forgot to say - they had advertised and hired two boys - in case one didn't show up - to carry our shoes and stuff so we could change for the wedding. They were out of work actors!

An all-glass room at the Met was reserved for the reception - beautiful tables, candles, string quartet, drinks, and a great variety of people meeting and greeting. We had the most gourmet dinner - four to choose from.

The next move was a get-together on the balcony of the Met. Kim and I stayed a short time. I listened to the groom's sister explain to me all the problems with her mattress, and her daughter who thought she was drunk. She had walked the entire mile in 4 inch heels with painted toes. Kim rescued me and we did the entire museum, including a rare show of modern - Noguchi, Barbara Hepworth, and a huge Joan Mitchell.

On Saturday we went to a Fun Market by Kim's apartment. Great neighbors with all their pets. She has a large park across the street with tennis courts, games, swimming, Kids Park and two main streets with neighborhood New Yorkers, and an elevator to the subway.

We attempted to do several things but couldn't make it work, so we hit Wall Street to see the Protestors. Dull! All the tents/people with tattoos and rings in lips, ears, eyebrows holding up signs and LOTS of tourists taking pictures. We did Starbucks and home, then hit the theatre scene - I chose to go to a "happening." No words, much meaning, if you wanted to interpret. I don't have the ability to describe in less than an hour, which is how long it lasted.

New York Slip / Brain Concussion

I slipped. I was visiting Kim Schultz in NY City and having a great time. Three days later, after seeing Fuerza Bruta (a wild theater happening), I got out of bed too quickly and slipped on Kim's well-polished Parkway wood floors. I saw both feet go high in the air, landing on my tailbone. I tried to grab the bed and HIT the back of my head on the corner of the windowsill. I can still hear the sound. It woke Kim from a sound sleep in the far other room and she came running. The neighbors upstairs heard the CRACK.

We called George. He was in aviation school classes in Kansas. He said, "Call an ambulance and get to the nearest hospital." Emergency room was packed. Skipping many hours, I had a concussion - blood or bleeding on the brain and was admitted to the hospital for two days. That's a whole book.

There were no "straight white" doctors or nurses - all nationalities and heavy accents. They called me "sweet love," "my girlie," "my strawberry blond sweetie." I had previously gotten a bad coloring job. Example of service - NO towels, NO toilet paper. I finally got an intern who brought me table napkins. He must have gotten them from a nearby cafe - NO soap and water. I shared the room with an aging woman who had many problems, who fell on her face. Her loud, Obnoxious Son (who never stopped talking) told his mother how he would take her home and would be there personally and get all the equipment she needed, BUT, at the last minute as they were packing, he said, "You're going to a Nursing Home." She cried, I cried, Kim who was with me cried.

I was on the side of a very large window overlooking lots of retired box cars, so I had a modern art gallery show with all the paintings. There were nurses in and out of many nationalities. An example of service was, I had signed three papers and a nurse picked one up. The doctor came to get all three. Well, they traced the third one to a nurse who had put it in her purse accidentally and had gone to church. The doctor's comment was, "Oh well!"

Among other drastic changes in my medicine, I was given two Benadryl. Four doctors and Kim and Randy were in my room. I suddenly saw Keith Haring drawings in three colors on the walls. I asked if others had seen them there before. Randy's face suddenly looked 100 years old, and I began to talk strangely. Randy jumped up and said, "She needs help, quick!" I was given something similar to the metal rings in your nose, only it was oxygen, and eventually the artwork went away. Someone said they usually don't give that medicine to anyone over 60. I asked, "Why me?" The doctor said, "I forgot you were over 21!" My records had read that I was in excellent shape for a woman of my age. I try to remember that. One doctor privately told me I was "a very pleasant, intelligent woman"! I hope I can remember that when I start teaching again.

Kim had constant calls to get George's OK on what to do. George questioned the medicine change except taking me off Coumadin to stop the bleeding. I didn't even know I had blood in my brain! I had to get out of there. George said to get out - stay at Kim's for a couple of days and he'd find someone to fly out and come home <u>by train</u> with me. Three doctors said it was ok by plane, and cheaper. The final doctor released me (under many terms) to stay 2 to 3 days in NY and come home by train <u>with someone</u>.

So, my wonderful caregivers grabbed the napkins (I had paid for) and took me back to Kim's apartment. Lots of phone calls and arrangements were made I didn't know about. Siobhan's musical was opening, Shari had two kids in school and husband Scott was in Kansas hunting - something - on my farm. I got a call from Sio saying <u>"I can, and I will fly to NY."</u> Despite her "Anything Goes" opening.

George (by phone between classes and tests) had put me back on my old formula of medicine in spite of the hospital. I really felt ok. Kim went to dinner with a friend who was hopefully going to give her her next big job - in India. Randy came over and cooked an elegant dinner. We had such fun. Actually, Randy's Central Park wedding and Met Museum Reception was my reason for the trip to NY.

Sio, heavy on Dramamine cause she's claustrophobic, was to arrive Saturday evening. Because she had missed her own show, I got us tickets to see "Anything Goes" on Broadway.

Saturday morning, Kim and I went to her Farmers Market near her apartment and got a good view of her neighborhood, people, and the huge park across the street, etc. Then she went to her yoga class, and I played. Still feeling ok, we headed out for a big NY City Day. Our list was long, but because of Subway Construction Problems, try as we did (using all elevators instead of steps for my sake), we couldn't get where we wanted to go or we would end up in Brooklyn (or was it the Bronx?). We gave up on our list and went to Wall Street to see the protesters' excitement. It was deadly dull. The park was filled with little tents and nice guys with tattoos and jewelry in their ears, nose, tongue, etc. standing around and a huge group of tourists walking around the tents taking photos. NOTHING. We hit Starbucks and headed home to get ready to meet Sio when she flew in. WELL, I developed a tight helmet pain in my head. Called George out of class! Back to the same hospital Emergency Room by cab this time.

Sio had arrived at the airport. Thank God for the cell phones. Kim directed her to take a bus to town from the airport, and I told her to go see the show 'cause Kim had to stay and manage me. It became complicated - Sio alone, it was dark, in the middle of NY. She had been directed to Kim's Apartment, but we were at the hospital Emergency Room with 40 desperate patients and one angry doctor.

Sio was on Dramamine and scared, with the subway directions too difficult to follow, so she called Shari in MN. Skipping details, Sio got her money back for our theatre tickets and got a cab ride to the hospital. He didn't know how to get there or wouldn't follow directions (I found this true of many NY taxi drivers). Much over-charged, Sio left him a 10-cent tip.

The three of us waited five hours through the night in the emergency room. The patients were rioting and shouting, "I'm going to die," "I need a doctor," "This is a waste of my Medicare," etc. Kim couldn't take it and blew up - some nurses calmed her and said to just take a breath. In the five hours I walked to the bathroom. The floor was covered with urine and patients were still yelling.

Kim found out the "man" doctor, who hated her, was going off duty. Different nurses had taken my vitals five times to keep me calm. The next doctor, "our savior," arrived. Kim grabbed him and brought him over to our stall, past patients who had waited eight hours. Wow! Kim, Sio, and I almost swooned. He was SO handsome - beautiful hair, voice, personality, and trapped at Mayo. He ordered another brain scan, HOWEVER, the machine was broken so it was the wildest, bumpy ride over to another hospital in an ambulance. The rollers didn't work on the bed. I mentioned the rough roads and pain. The driver told me to call the mayor to fix the road! It was good to be out in fresh (almost) air after that 5-hour experience.

They couldn't slide me to the scanning machine. I made them move it, unstrap me, and thank goodness for my long legs, I climbed onto the scan machine. The bleeding had stopped. Dr. Handsome told us the brain doctor (who hadn't seen me - so busy) insisted I go back to the hospital for a week. Kim called George. Dr. George talked to Dr. Handsome. George asked, "If this was your mother..." A round about conversation went on. Dr. Handsome <u>had to</u> say what the trained brain doctor had said. They thought I could fly home, Dr. George said, "No." I got ready to leave at 5 am. I signed a paper saying I wouldn't sue, etc. He told me privately that if I had any problems to come back, and what to do about Medicare. Sio was taking notes and felt terribly torn about me leaving the hospital - between the brain doctor and George. George over the phone was saying, "<u>Just Do It.</u>"

We chose to escape from the rioting patients. Before I left the emergency room, Kim and I were on our way to another cleaner bathroom she had found. Dr. Handsome stopped us and said, "Would you mind giving me a urine sample?" With a tilt of his head, he winked, smiled, and walked away. We giggled and agreed we'd give him our urine for the rest of our lives!

Back to Kim's and "fix" the medicine, Sio got to see Kim's beautiful apartment and pack. We slept (sort of), then took the subway to 59th and a cab across town, and stopped to see Christmas windows. We went into my favorite Bergdorf Goodman. The three of us with luggage and travel clothes looking at expensive clothes and shoes, $4500, and taking photos of the decor. How sophisticated!

We crossed into another most beautiful shop, took pictures, and went in where beautifully elegant clerks were "nicely" wanting us to purchase candles, cosmetics etc. A neat, smooth black clerk, in a $5000 English cut suit, grabbed both my hands and was SO excited. He said a top make-up artist I had never heard of was a special guest there. I needed a little color; would I be a model? Ugh, one artist had worked on a customer's left eye lid for 10 minutes applying different shades of blue. We got a cab back to the train station carrying our bags of food, and with lots of help from Kim, we boarded. Sio took her Dramamine for her claustrophobia, and we found our way to our sleeper and settled in for our 36-hour ride back to Winona.

Summer Trip to Visit Paul Fusillo

What a Summer! A week in the Blue Ridge Mountains of North Carolina with a mother bear and her two cubs sauntering by, and dinner with $90 wines. Then a week in Denver at a Theater Convention with Siobhan. We found five hours to play at all the high spots together (101 degrees) and Sio dancing with a gorgeous harem dancer at the Marrakesh. Now in Oregon. Lots of time with George's mother (age 93) and impossible brother. The beach house is unavailable, so we escaped to Shakespeare Festival and through the Redwood Forest Mountains to travel up the seacoast, with many stops and memories of doing the trip with the girls 37 years ago.

Hours of conversation – Paul's many stories are so fun. Classical music - Haydn, on the TV Dulcie's present, coffee pot always serving quietly and slowly. Tree cut off so it wouldn't block views. Paul and I decided he needed a little bear sitting cross legged there reading the newspaper. Story of fish pond and Paul getting snipper for dead leaves. 101 Revlon – ordered 10. Paul wants a little goat for a pet.

Paul's many stories – diamond ring for Dulcie, $50,000. 1.2 million – $10,000 a month for 5 years for boys. All troubles with Alice – endless, info for Dulcie of family's first meal out, penne, dried tomato, olives, spinach nuts. College aged young waiter enamored by me. Got iced tea in Wine glass, writing on the porch - second dinner out – wine $80.

Paul proposed for Christmas to stay here – have Christmas, then go to Tampa condo to avoid asthma sickness. Have everyone here – 30 people. Paul told stories of Ronnie and his wedding. Parents Catholic, Paul's great clothes – sporty and expensive. Always suspenders.

St. Patrick's Day

The Chicago River was no longer green but had turned back to black. I had not finished my green velvet jacket I was creating and forgot to bring the HUGE green ball ring Santha gave me. I did get a hug from a leprechaun and a gold coin,

BUT...

the point of my trip to Chicago was to see Siobhan in a Woody Allen play - the lead role of a character I couldn't believe she could do, with a New Jersey accent (A+), every mannerism (A+), reaction (A+), looks (A+) - she was unrecognizable as Siobhan - the *professional actress.*

The Steel Beam Theatre is up a flight of stairs (I'm just recovering from a broken foot and broken shoulder - much pain), and we went to the theatre two hours early for prep. There was one chair in the lobby I could sit in for 2 hours - or go to a better spot - next door was an Irish pub. Inside the pub was filled but outdoors on a patio were some 150 people who had started drinking beer early.

I decided to wander over and people watch, rather than sit in the lobby chair. I had drifted to the edge of the crowd (all wearing green something). I hoped to be unnoticed. There were tables and chairs and a long counter with stools - all filled. As I approached, a very handsome young (40) man leaned over and announced, "You are a beautiful lady. I will give you my stool." He then tried several times - conversation and asked several times - my name. He finally got Viv, so he announced in a most theatrical voice, "Hey everyone, this is Viv!" Someone said, "Let's all drink to Viv!!" All the different groups continued their drunken chatter. Five different people tried to buy me a beer. One said, "Please, just once." I said, "No." One more drunk said, "Aww," as he almost fell off his stool.

I stayed 1½ hours watching all the different groups get very drunk. Some wanted to take my picture (without a camera). I finally snuck away and slowly climbed the stairs up to the one-chair theatre lobby, and sat until the theatre opened.

THEN

What a surprise! Siobhan was unrecognizable as a Jewish mother and wife with an authentic Jewish accent. She is SO professional. One scene with her tangled with another, trying to untangle, was a Show Stopper. What timing! She was attempting to get something out of the other's back pocket and they slowly twisted around and around and ended up on the floor, she with one leg straight up. Wow. The audience screamed with laughter.

After the show, she finally came out with make-up off and hair *flowing* around her. She was So Glamorous. I only wished I could have seen the show again.

What a wonderful St Patrick's Day trip - and to think I almost canceled because of aches, pains, and transportation issues. SO, LUCKY I decided to go for it!

The Trip - New York 2013

The New York trip was packed with wonders. I'm amazed I can still handle it - well, with help from Sio. We saw three Broadway shows. "Peter the Sky Catcher" was everything Theatre is **or should be.** Saw Tom Hanks plus four people from my favorite show, Law & Order.

We went to the most expensive shops. Scarves were $600. Sio tried on $2000 shoes that didn't fit. A gorgeous 6' black clerk brought us leather dresses to look at - $12,000. Bergdorf Goodman (the most) had two tall, skinny models roaming about. We joined a cocktail and chocolate party with racks of thousands of $$ of evening dresses. No champagne but the chocolates were delicious. We became very critical of designs!

We did SoHo and all the boutiques. Art galleries, museums,

people watching and found a gorgeous work of art - a BIG neck-lace in an exotic boutique. Sio got the price reduced. In another boutique I got earrings and a silver, flat, round ring - 1½" wide. We "did" the fabric district looking for "straw" material for Rumpelstiltskin. We found it for pants, and a gorgeous dark gold sequin for a draped top. It'll be wild "constructing it" AND wearing it!

The best part was a 3-hour lunch with my ex-4th grade student I "taught" 55 years ago. She has written a musical with a possible producer for Broadway. She told Sio all about my teaching, with tons of compliments and surprises. I didn't know what to do for Phy. Ed. so they did the Can-Can. She remembered so many wonderful details and covered me with compliments about my "methods." I'm so lucky to get to hear this 50 + years later. I think she made up some for the effect.

Sio stopped at every street scarf shop to look for a certain color scarf. I was weary from carrying that HEAVY necklace. I asked the old man who spoke no English who was sitting on a chair by a scarf stall if I could sit on his lap, and he motioned that his knees hurt but he got up and I sat.

In Times Square with the leftover SLUSH, I was dancing with Elmo. And from a block away, this wild haired woman came shouting, "VIVIAN!" It was Gretchen from our department at WSU.

That day made National News. Another dressed comic character was having his photo taken with a young boy. The mother didn't tip him - he knocked her down - she sued.

This was very different from my last NY trip when I slipped on a highly polished floor and got a concussion and Sio flew out to bring me home on a LONG train ride.

Chicago Weekend

Siobhan drove to Winona and picked me up and we drove - she drove, I slept - to Chicago (well near) Wednesday and finally found Kim's apartment *and* actually found a *tight* parking space.

What a wonderful apartment, and such a Hostess!! She is so kind and generous - cooked a great Italian dinner - lots of talk and directions for Siobhan - what to do about her pet cat, keys, etc, etc. Kim said she would be gone early Thursday morning for storytelling in Nebraska.

Sio planned and organized everything. We took an Uber into Chicago and played all day and came by another fun Uber. It was my first time using Uber. The driver was 'foreign' and friendly. We stopped to pick up another and all started talking. The driver said he was an actor, the other guest said he was a stage manager.

Sio said she was an actress, and I couldn't think of what I was, so Sio helped and told them I was a director. After that I got much attention from the "out-of-work" theatre people.

Friday was wonderful. We explored boutiques, fashion, food, and I saw her show. Saturday, she drove part way, and George met us in my car and headed back Home. I felt as if I'd at least been to Europe.

Memories of NYC Trip with Siobhan

Compliments

While Sio was looking and talking "details" of an expensive purse, the handsome clerk thought I was wearing a "Barry" necklace – a jewelry designer. Three clerks (separately) complimented my jewelry, one thought my ring was coral - she had never seen coral that big. Two people asked if they could photograph my necklace (it's made from a parrot toy at the pet shop for $11.50).

An Italian woman with a straight American man threw him her big purse and RAVED about beauty - and mother and daughter - over and over. We were sitting by the large water fountain.

A short man, well-dressed carrying enormous packages from the most expensive shops, walking in front of us, turned, and raved about mother and daughter - beauty - "the way to live life" - he had terrible teeth. He was a Delivery Man - How peasant of us to think he had purchased.

Sio told the stewardess on the plane about my award. Tall, handsome, black steward said he loved my ring. He said "It really fits your personality." This was when I was waiting for the toilet.

Space/Buildings

I'm so aware of space - that's how I design clothes - how to reshape the space of my body. We were in the middle of all different, all magnificent, beautifully shaped skyscrapers, and the one so universal looked like a kid had colored it with pale crayons of four colors right out our window.

I was leaning against a wall (5th Avenue) and the crowd walking toward us was totally unaware of each other. One woman walked past me so close she stepped on my feet!

People

Two black girls with elaborate hair braiding. One girl told me it took four hours to braid it and cost $200.

Hard, short woman with a perfume sample - Channel - said, "We already gave you one," she said to Barb who was standing there.

A male model "built" in just shorts, ironing an orange cloth for a wash and wear ad in a room of several cosmetic booths. I wished I had put my skirt up on the ironing board for my Christmas card.

It was Very Hot so I went to Henri Bendel's to wait for Barb. A woman found a velvet, gold trimmed chair for me - I went out to tell Sio where I was, came back in - a man took it so she put me on an elegant display sofa, up curved steps and I was there when Barb and Bob came in, and Barb shouted, "Vivian!" across the room.

It was 80 degrees, 86 humidity and Sio was outside endlessly arguing with Barb that that wasn't the address for Henri B (it had moved). She and Bob were by our hotel out "walking fast" to meet us, going by the Plaza Hotel by Central Park. I remember when I took the train in from Long Island (Mrs. Fusillo home) to quickly walk around and take in the city by myself. I always stopped by the Plaza, sat, and listened to a string quartet before I took the train back to Long Island.

The van driver was nice (I sat in front), and I mentioned the park. He asked if I wanted to go through it. This was on our long, winding side street ride back to the airport. Sio sat in the back, and I yelled, "Sio, I want that lamp in the window," as we passed a beautiful furniture store. He said, "Shall I stop and put it in the back?" I told him he was a very nice man. He smiled and said, "Sometimes, not always." The trip took so long that a guy behind me said, "I wanna go home."

This driver (and atmosphere) was in complete contrast to the angry driver who picked us up at the airport to take us into the city. He shouted and honked at every one and ranted about what a terrible airport LaGuardia was. The man who complimented me and my necklace in the Henri Bendel shop earlier had changed positions and was at the door to leave and stopped us to say, "Don't you remember me?"

Times Square

Just 2 blocks from the Edison Hotel, we found a place to sit for "people looking." Hundreds taking "selfies," some with 3 ft. and 6 ft. extensions. So many women in high heels - no more wedges, but tiny heels that stuck in floor openings.

The usual Statue of Liberty, Mickey and Minnie Mouse, etc. - characters dressed to have photos taken for tips. The Statue of

Liberty guys were 10 feet tall on stilts (a memory of Richard Esvang playing the witch wearing stilts).

We purchased our food in the restaurant/grocery store one door down, open all night, and took it to a different place to eat - Rockefeller Center, Radio City Music Hall, Times Square, etc.

The big, exciting purchase was blush and lipstick. I had a case with a tiny rim of black I bought 45 years ago. I've never sat at a cosmetic counter and had various shades tested on me. Quite an experience under the guide of Sio. The other returned to the shop with many booths of various brands to see. A very pretty girl with long, black eye lashes told me I had pretty lips, (good sales pitch) and with Sio's guidance we purchased the Bestest shade. A first for me.

Of the hundreds of fashionable clothes at very high prices, I didn't see any I'd buy or want to wear. Did see some great designs and many I've seen in magazines. A rust lattice long dress with pleated skirt, $10,000. I liked it, but I'd want to cut off the skirt and make pants.

After a 3-hour lunch with Barb and Bob at a French Bistro, we decided we should pack before the show, American in Paris. I wanted to go to the most expensive Bergdorf Goodman for fashion. Barb said, "We want to go with you if we won't spoil your style." Sio parted and found some classy plain, and Barb picked all wild ones and shouted, "Vivian, you'd look great in this." Lots of hugs and we parted. She had a 2½ hour train ride back to Jersey.

Other Shops

Amazing - such a lot of expensive space to display a single dress or a belt. One shop had two Gorgeous Boys at the front door, then another just inside and three or four girls to sell - all dressed in black. I found a window seat to "sit," but the clerk insisted I sit on a beautiful, white little sofa. They offered us **WINE** "to celebrate." We don't drink so they brought us a beautiful goblet of ice water in a saucer. Went to another shop with beautiful clerks in really ugly red dresses, no customers and the toilet didn't flush.

One day, I thought I should wear my tennis shoes - I got a swollen, painful ankle. We couldn't get a cab so we walked home. Sio got ice and surrounded my ankle with it up on a pillow. I fell asleep. And Sio had a little time to herself to try to find some presents. I really regret that she didn't have more time to be alone. I should have been exercising much more before the trip.

We had our morning croissant and coffee upstairs in Radio City where there was an Architects' Convention. Got a seat with a young man. So beautifully groomed who majored in architecture at N.Y.U. We talked about Bailey.

With the cancellations of our plane, we had extra time, so after Sio made all the phone calls to cancel my Rochester connection and have George pick me up in Minneapolis, we got a cab to the Museum of Modern Art. Because of the rain, it was packed. I got a glimpse of some wonderful art and we found presents in the bookstore. Magic - many colored pencils I purchased - a square piece of wood when you touch it said the time and temp for George.

American in Paris was perhaps the best musical ever. The choreography propelled scenery, different periods of costumes, dances - Powerful. We were on our way to our seats, the usher stopped me to compliment my earrings.

There was a big "stir" down front and lots of cameras. I asked the woman next to me and she said, "It's Bill." It was Bill Clinton. At intermission he came up the aisle, kissed an elderly lady (not me), signed autographs, and SMILED. I was 3 ft. from him. I think he was going to the bathroom. Coming back in he was stopped by tons of cameras, and what looked like a veteran lecturing him. Anyway, he couldn't sit so the conductor had to start the music with many still standing. I'm glad Sio got a magnet for memory.

Returning to Winona from New York Trip - The Adventure!

Craig called and said he *really* needed me to come to NY. Steve, his roommate, was sick, so he'd arranged for me to stay in a friend's apartment nearby - name of Paul. SO, I reorganized fast and went. We had a wonderful day together and I went to meet Paul, a really nice guy - musician.

Craig had found an interesting place for coffee. We walked and talked blocks to lower West Side to 6th Ave, to where MTV was shooting the movie, Slaves of New York. We talked and walked back to his apartment. Steven, his roommate, was asleep. Craig got a flashlight to get through his black bedroom, lit only by the huge fish tank the width of his double bed, to the front room. I scooched against the mirrored wall to see the videos and make decisions. A call came in from an MTV writer for a new character to shoot a movie audition that pm. We spent hours planning his video audition, taking cuts from all his tapes and movies. It was great to be his director again.

This story is about coming back to Winona, or <u>Getting from</u> <u>NY airport to Winona:</u>

I thought I had plenty of time, even dawdled around trying to find Sio a graduation card. I said goodbye to Paul and thanked him, and took a taxi to Port Authority. CAREY bus was outside but not loading so I went to the lady's room, opened the stall door, and saw a girl who looked like Santha lying on the floor. I ran to get help - a policewoman came and told me to leave the building, or I'd be stuck in a court case. She'd take care of it.

I got in the Carey Bus, and we got to Grand Central - Big Delays. Our bus driver was something - gave lectures on every question asked - talk, talk, talk, TENSION RISING - the others had more time before their plane, and <u>they</u> were wrecks. I told a few when my flight was, and all said, "You Won't Make It!" - non-refundable ticket - Get A Cab! FINALLY, I got off the bus, got my ticket back (with a lecture and had to get my suitcase off - way in the back and impossible - ran into the station - got money refund on ticket - (not easy), found my suitcase and waved a cab, asked how much to the airport, he said $40. Would he take a Traveler's Check? No. SO, I went in and bought another bus ticket - put my suitcase on and got another lecture from the driver and eventually we were off - TENSION HIGH with everyone, *and* he made 3 stops before mine. FINALLY got to the Pan Am Domestic and went by it and around to Pan Am International.

I really had to go to the bathroom. Should I give up? I must - no choice - The plane is GONE. Now the BATTLE. First the bathroom. Going from a long line of angry people waiting to see whether they were in the right line - no assistance anywhere - just yelling. I left one line twice and had to start over.

I realized I must contact George, who was getting ready to fly to Minneapolis that very minute to meet me - Where to Phone? In the Pan Am building after much panicking, I found a total of 10 phones - all broken but two, and a long line waiting. Each time I had to go through security to get to the phone line, my metal bracelet kept setting off the buzzer. I reached George just in the nick of time. Well, 4 hours of this and I went from, "I could go to the other building and try to get a flight," - NO WAY - or I could pay $75 and get on standby. I KEPT TRYING. I finally found a clerk and told my story of finding the girl - maybe dead - in the Port Authority. She said, "You couldn't make up such a story. I'll see what I can do." She got me on a flight HOME - no added money - tomorrow morning - next day - same time. 20 hours away. I took it. I had fought a major war and won.

Where to check my baggage overnight? I assumed lockers like in Minneapolis. NO. I went to another building, checked with security and they were filled. I pleaded one more time - OK. I phoned Shari - not home, George - not home, Steve Geck - not home, Craig - left a message on his answering machine, Paul - the machine. He had gone out after I said goodbye.

I could do no more but enjoy the city some more, so I bussed back to the Port Authority, taxied to Paul's house, the door was locked, and I had given him my key. It was 10 pm. I sat on his front steps. I watched all the street life - dog walkers, a charming Italian firing up his van, gay couples. I went to the corner to get a drink. I tried all phones again. Garrison Keillor, who lived next door, came back from a show he did and invited me in, but I said no. It was a beautiful, cool night. Paul came home and found me curled in a ball by the door - AMAZED.

I said bye to Paul once again. I got a bagel to take on the plane and started OVER, 4 hours early. Paul told me to take the

Kennedy Express, but I was afraid of New Stuff so train to 42nd to Port Authority, Carey bus to Kennedy, stop at Grand Central, met a nice lady from Australia (now I know it all), got my bag out of checking, rolled it over to counter to check bags - PLENTY OF TIME.

Off to Gate 20, sat down to write this and enjoy - realize I didn't have a seat assignment, so up to the counter and ANOTHER BATTLE. I had to take the People Carrier to another gate. Pan Am had purchased from Northwest? I held onto a stewardess from St. Olaf who was going to Minneapolis for 7 days. We entered a Big Strange Building - NO guiding signs - foreigners and others lost. Not One clear speaking white person on any microphones to make announcements. WHAT A MESS! We had to change gates again. I held onto my stewardess friend. When I got my seat assignment - TAGS to my luggage FLEW OUT. She said it didn't matter, in Minneapolis they'd take care of it.

Easy trip to Minneapolis - So easy, So clean, So friendly. I could handle anything. Next Episode: Getting to Winona. The adjustment is much less difficult coming this way. I know I'm home. The people all bend forward to help. It's SO clean. It's so quiet I hear every bird's new song outside my window. When I arrived, I covered the entire town, talked to all the people I knew, told bits of stories about the Neverland I had just returned from. I biked around the lake while Shari ran, looking up at the sailboats almost to tip over, and getting deep whiffs of our rose gardens. We took our salad lunch to the Mississippi and sat on the gorgeous dikes and watched a big barge go by, water skiers getting out of the way just in time, waved to friendly people on the occasional boats out for the day.

I made a trip in my yellow convertible to Northwest Fabric. I stop in daily for my therapy to design fabric and go away with at least one piece of fabric to add to my full basement of stuff I'm going to do 'someday.' Northwest Fabrics is CLOSED. A rush of excitement will soon be. Summer school begins at 7:30 - 11:30 and that's a workout. We're going to a chicken barbecue this afternoon...a crowd of pilots and owners of their homemade planes will have a 'do' at a nearby town where a friend has his own private airport, then stop and pick strawberries on the way home. We have tickets for the historical Society Dance...another type of conversation, this weekend friends are coming from Maine. I'll meet them in Minneapolis, stay over with Santha, and take her to the opening at the Guthrie, and it's just 5 weeks until my trip to Spain, Portugal, and Morocco!

Part Six

TEACHING AND LIFE

In a Class all her Own

Published in the Winona Post, Apr 2, 2015
   by AMELIA WEDEMEYER

In her living room on a Thursday afternoon, Vivian Fusillo spoke of her love of jewelry, including the personal collection she has amassed over the 65 years she spent as a teacher. While the pieces in Fusillo's collection range in color and size, as well as origin — from the barren lands of Russia to the monsoon regions of India — each one is different, bursting with its own personality, much like Fusillo herself. "Almost all of my jewelry is from my students," she explained, including the two large amber-colored rings on her fingers. "Each has a novel behind it."

This March, Fusillo, who retired from Winona State University (WSU) last May, received another gift from a student. Yet, instead of a new brooch or pendant to add to her collection of baubles, Fusillo was one of 13 recipients across the country honored with a 2015 Kennedy Center/Stephen Sondheim Inspirational Teacher Award. Through a nomination by a former student, the award recognizes teachers who have had a significant impact on the lives of their students both inside and outside the classroom. "I was in total shock," Fusillo remembered. "In fact, I am in shock and I am amazed. Mostly, it's the excitement of having a student [who would recognize my work]." Although most of Fusillo's years teaching were spent in theater departments and auditoriums, the award honors a year early in her career as a teacher, when she taught inside a cramped classroom with no air conditioning some 60 years ago. "I taught one year in fourth grade in what was called a 'Strawberry School,'" she explained. In the first half of the 20th century, Florida's "Strawberry Schools" were schools intended for children of poor families that could not afford extra help to farm. The schools closed when harvest time came around so that students could spend that time helping their parents pick strawberries and various fruit. "I'm sure they had never seen anything like me before," Fusillo said with a smile.

In her letter nominating Fusillo for the Kennedy Center/Stephen Sondheim award, Barbara Hustedt Cook, who was one of those 40 fourth-grade students, talked about how her former teacher was unafraid to learn from her students as much as her students learned from her. "By taking her cue from us, with her trademark joy and pizazz, she gave us the confidence to go with our own interests and strengths, wherever they might take us, all the way," Hustedt Cook wrote, "in my case, from random words and sentences to a story of continuing growth that isn't done yet. And if that's not what it is to inspire, I don't know what is."

"It was a wonderful year," Fusillo recalled. She taught with enthusiasm and creativity, using methods that went beyond opening up a standard textbook and reading aloud to a classroom. "We started all kinds of things," Fusillo explained. To teach her students how to speak in front of an audience, she set an oatmeal box on a tripod and had the children talk as if they were anchors recording the nightly news. Another activity involved Fusillo's students contorting their bodies to letters of the alphabet, spelling out words with accompanying punctuation marks. "Anything I could do [to engage them]," she said. If it's any indication of how much her students looked up to her in the brief time she spent in the small classroom in the 1955-1956 school year, it's in the subtleties. Like the students who would come after them, many of her Strawberry School children became enamored with Fusillo's unique aura. "All the boys made big rings because I wore them," Fusillo remembered.

Although her time with the Strawberry School students was brief, lasting only a year, Fusillo stayed in contact with some of her former students, including Hustedt Cook, whom she plans to visit in New York this summer. "She's recently written a musical, which she hopes to get produced fairly soon off-Broadway," Fusillo explained, referring to Hustedt Cook. "She has done a lot, and she would have done it without me, but she gives me credit."

After her year at the Strawberry School, Fusillo went on to become the head of the theater department at Florida Southern College, and later spent time at Stephen F. Austin State University and Western Illinois University before settling in Winona as a professor at WSU. Fusillo can still recall the day she was hired in 1968; she met Robert A. DuFresne, the president of WSU at the time, while he was playing cello. Soon after she was introduced to the dean and hired on the spot. "That's when I started, and I forgot to leave," Fusillo said.

In her 46 years at WSU, Fusillo has inspired the lives of many of her students as well as a few who never had a class with her, but were nonetheless captivated by her presence. One of those students was burgeoning screenwriter Mark Steven Johnson, who attended WSU before graduating from California State University, Long Beach. "He was always nearby; I knew who he was, but he wasn't in theater," Fusillo said. Johnson, who is originally from Hastings, left WSU and moved out west to complete his degree and went on to eventually write "Grumpy Old Men" and its sequel, "Grumpier Old Men."

As some already know, Fusillo was the inspiration behind the enchanting Ariel Truax character, played by Ann Margaret in the original film. "She underplays it so much," commented Fusillo's daughter, Shari. Even now, Fusillo is coy when asked about the movies and the character. Fusillo insists that besides the red hair and a few whimsical traits, such as enjoying making snow angels in fresh snow, she and her character aren't one and the same. Though she did admit, "I was overwhelmed that the character would be [modeled] after me."

After teaching

Now a full-time retiree, Fusillo is having a hard time adjusting to life outside of teaching. She's likened retirement to finally "graduating" from her teaching career, although the desire to continue leading and inspiring young people has not faded. "I'm not capable of just doing nothing," she said. "I'm always visiting students from my past — they're actually saving me." Shari agreed, adding that her mother's relationships with her former students are what keeps her going. "She has had such a hard time retiring," Shari said, "[so she] likes to travel and visit all these students and hear about their lives. I think the big thing is that students believe she has inspired them, but she is also inspired by them a lot, too."

Portrait of Me

My portrait, painted by Julie Johnston, is hanging at the Blue Heron – with a light on it.

Every day I hear how beautiful, how lovely it is. How she's caught my real beauty, etc, etc.

I feel so lucky in every way (in spite of nightmares). I feel like a little girl from Bogue, Kansas who knows 'nothing,' about 40 years old who is playing 'dress up' at the Acoustic. I'm so thankful for the amazing close family I get to be with, and living with George is beyond description. He cares for all of us so deeply.

A Brief History of My "No Goals" Life:

I never seem to have goals - I'm pushed into a situation and somehow make it work.

1. My first time on stage, 3rd grade, pushed by my mother into singing and dancing at PTA.

2. In between acts doing Judy Garland songs at intermission with traveling Tobey Players who came to Bogue once a month. I also did a chalk drawing to music. I have NO idea how that happened.

3. Mother arranged for us to move to Salina, KS. To pay bills, I got a waitress job - made LOTS OF TIPS from soldiers on leave - had the best tables to work. I had only helped Mrs. Trombley in Bogue.

4. Push to go to Marymount - STATE. Majored in business. Did a show so NUNS established a theatre major for me.

5. Sent to Catholic U in DC summers to study with Walter Kerr, Jean Kerr, and Allen Schneider because my theatre teacher had been there. It was WAR TIME - I had never traveled alone

anywhere. I took a train, got off near Catholic U and walked. Someone watering their lawn accidentally sprayed me - and needed someone to share a house.

6. I took a class with Jean Kerr. She was writing Our Hearts were Young and Gay, Walter Kerr directed. I was put in charge of costumes and got to go to Boston with lead actress Cornelius Skinner to collect them.

7. I needed to find a job, but where? How? I got a phone call (a mistaken number) that I got the job and could choose my hours. It was waitressing at the Metropolitan Club where all-stars, elites, politicians, etc. frequented. Because I was the only college kid, the boss proudly introduced me to many. I had never heard of some, including The Rockefellers. Mrs. seemed very excited to meet me. I didn't know what to say so I said, "I saw your place in NY City with the skating rink."

8. I met Bob. He was in charge of entertainment at the Air Base and I at Marymount. I needed a truck load of men for the big dance. After that evening we were cast leads in several plays. My father died after a long cancer fight my senior year just before my senior recital. So many debts. (I went to NY City to meet the Fusillos.)

9. My mother went back to college for teaching credits and we both took jobs at Formosa, KS. She was grade school principal and I taught typing, bookkeeping, sewing in charge of cheer-leaders and started theatre (many stories here). Bob and I got married at Easter, age 21 and he taught 1 year in a country school grades 1-5.

10. 1 stayed teaching high school for 5 years, and he went to Hays, KA to get a degree. Summer, I took Art and he and I were leads in huge plays.

11. While standing in line we looked down, and in the waste-basket was a form to apply for a scholarship to Europe to study. We decided to try. Neither of us spoke any languages but English, so it had to be England - Stratford-Upon-Avon. He was accepted at the Shakespeare Institute with 11 scholars around the world. Every break we hitchhiked all over Europe - even to see Queen Elizabeth crowned. I went to design school. We visited all top 60's artists and saw hundreds of plays. We were written up in newspapers and photo in LIFE Magazine.

12. The theatre costume crowd were having tea, and I sat across the room wanting to meet them. They were doing Richard III and had 50 some costumes to create - fast. They asked me if I designed my clothes and could I come help sew - no pay - but with all top designers and acting company of John Gielgud, Laurence Olivier, Peggy Ashcroft, Richard Burton, and Alec Guinness, etc, etc. Guthrie was there planning to start a theatre in Minneapolis. I had a wonderful time. Bob was big into photography.

13. So many hitch-hiking adventures. In Bogue I don't think I heard of Europe.

14. Bob's father died. He debated returning to New York - little money. One passport for all 3 of us, so Santha and I stayed in England. While he was gone, I was talking to rich tourists at the theatre and told them my problems. They loaned me the money!

15. It was time to get a job at home. Bob applied (PhD not completed). He was told by agents he couldn't get American jobs with his beard. Had a tweed suit. Dr. Spivey at Fla. Southern who went to Japan with a seat next to Frank Lloyd Wright and arrived home had talked Wright into designing the campus. His application was accepted, and on the highway with all the traffic, he

phoned Spivey who said, (it was a Methodist college) "Do you go to church? We can't have any atheists here." Bob said he directed a church choir once - good enough. We had been staying with Mrs. F and Paul and had $100. So, Paul found us a $100 Hudson and we were on our way.

16. A teacher was needed for 4th grade at a very poor 'strawberry school' near Lakeland. This is the story of the award nominated by Barb, one of my students!!!

17. Dr. Spivey used Bob and I to help entertain his guests every Sunday evening. He told me to come see him. I thought I'd have to direct some rich ladies for a big donation and didn't go for 2 weeks. (Another big story.) When I finally went, he said, "I want you to be Head of the Theatre." By that time, we had told my mother to quit teaching and moved her to Lakeland. So, we both taught at Florida Southern and returned to Europe every summer. Bob was fired after 4 years. He went to Tampa. I taught there 5.

18. Bob was fired and got a job at Nacogdoches, Texas. Twins were born. Edith was his student. He moved out. He was fired, and she graduated. They left for Atlanta, GA. I got my Masters. NOW I HAD A GOAL.

I had to find a job. I applied everywhere for speech, theatre, costume, Oral Interp, whatever! I had several interviews across the U.S. and was flown there but wouldn't get the job. Finally, a friend said, "Something's wrong. I'll look at your resume." It said, 'She's been through so much - when she recovers, she'll be a great teacher.' He removed that and I got a job over the phone with an exclusive school in California. I was scared and got a lawyer to break the contract. Ugh. I went to Minneapolis for an interview - I was picked up in a hearse by the Dean. The back had cushions and liquor etc. - NoGood. At the U, I walked back and forth looking for a room number for my interview. A prof was sitting outside - I said, "Excuse me," every time I passed him. Finally I asked, "Are you going to sit there all day?" He invited me to sit down. I told him my whole sad story. He knew a perfect job opening for me in a beautiful little town, great for my 3 little girls to grow up in (and then we could move to NY, he thought). He called Miss Magnus. I got the job, sight unseen. Got the girls, arrived in my VW convertible, and we began - I forgot to leave. Someone said, "You're just waiting for the next accident." Amazing.

Griffin School Story

You should see our Science Table. I'm amazed. We have a rock collection. A bowl of tadpoles - one is getting legs. When it becomes a frog, we'll put it in our terrarium with Molasses (our little turtle that really has a personality). It eats out of the kids' hands. Barbara (my NY genius) brought in a mud snake about 6 inches long - all excited - telling me all the information about it and said, "While I get it home ready would you hold it?" and *handed it to me.* I was amazed I wasn't scared. It (Egghert is his name) gets fed milk, and at morning break it goes outside around Barbara's wrist. We also have a little catfish and two goldfish.

Monday, I promised them we would do a class newspaper. I got some colored ditto papers donated to me. Last week I had a short story contest and I got three really marvelous stories with all spelling and punctuation correct. Next week is the poetry contest. All this is for my real advanced students.

I'm the Red Cross Representative and 2 girls are the Junior Representatives. We have a meeting once a month, make tray favors for the hospitals and lots of helpful things they love to do. For Art everyone designed a big kite with good results. Last time we had a quiz and Barbara won. Also got her picture taken for the paper (a little publicity).

Teaching Grade School in Florida

The kids love me even when I punish them, and I'm really strict, but they love it. They've never had any art or pretty colors in their life (very poor), and I've collected supplies from all over and they're really good and neat with it. I put brown paper on the wall completely around the room and it's covered with painted circus people, tents, and animals. I have some that do 8th grade reading, so I now have a table and chairs for the reading club. I discovered a moldy globe, and they love Geography now. I have them read aloud a lot with expression and have endless arithmetic drills (I hate arithmetic).

I made one boy stay after school to finish his work, and the next night four long faced kids were outside my door asking why they couldn't stay in. They tell me they've never had to work so hard before, but they like it. I'll use the writing hint, any material to be used for a little program is *really* welcome. We have one once a month.

I told them the other day that if every time I gave an assignment they didn't do it right, they got 'F' and would stay in the 4th grade another year. They all shouted they wanted to if I would be their teacher. One boy who knew who I meant stood up and said, "No sir, I'm the only one that gets to stay here with Mrs. Fusillo."

The Strawberry School

We had lived in England and had many adventures hitchhiking through Europe, and Bob had finished his class work and could write his thesis anywhere. We considered living on the Riviera but after many inquiries it wasn't possible, so we needed to get home, get jobs, pay off debts and hope to return to England during summers, SO...Bob joined agencies, had photos taken with his well-groomed beard and lots of recommendations. The agency said, "No one will hire you in the US with a beard." We were living in New York with Mrs. Fusillo and Paul and doing work (we completed her attic). We decided to get on the road to see my mother, and with our $100, Paul found us a car.

The only inquiry he got was from Dr. Spivey at Florida Southern in Lakeland, who was a very off-the-norm experimental president who had gotten a seat on a plane next to Frank Lloyd Wright, who was going to Japan to watch a certain flower bloom, and by the time he got home he had talked FLW into designing the whole campus.

We were speeding down the highway and Bob stopped by a side-of-the-road phone and called Spivey, with noise from the trucks going by. Spivey asked him if he went to church, because it was a religious college, and he couldn't have any atheists. Bob paused and said, "Well, I once directed a church choir." That was enough and we were on our way. We arrived in the Florida heat with our $100 car - we had to decide whether we wanted the windows up or down - permanently. We arrived and found we were the youngest on campus. Everyone was retired professors from the north.

Bob, with his folk singing performances, soon became Spivey's favorite to show off with guests, like when Eleanore Roosevelt arrived, and many others. To back up - word got out about me. There was a 4th grade teacher at a country 'Strawberry School' who needed to quit, and I was asked to fill in. I told them not for a week or so. We needed to drive to Kansas to see my mother, pick up our STUFF and I needed to learn SOME-THING about teaching 4th grade.

On the way to Kansas, I kept looking at schools and wondered what a 4th grader looked like. I had not taken a single education class - NO teaching certification, NO experience. My Mother was teaching at the time. I went to school with her, and she provided teaching tips for me to use.

We returned to Florida, Bob in the English Department, and I drove to the Strawberry School. What a Shock! There were 40 in the classroom - wall to wall - no air conditioning - all very poor with terrible family problems. The only art was a huge picture of a foot hanging in the front of the room with a hook worm crawling in the toe!! The principal was a FIRM woman who had a strap and told me, "These kids are rotten. If they don't behave, just send them to me, I'll strap 'em." I had to eat with them, so I cut and shampooed their hair. We had peanut butter balls Every Day for dessert. I began knowing Nothing. I decided I knew Nothing about Normal Teaching so the other teachers would have to handle all that, and I'd do what I could to expose them to Art, Beauty, Manners, etc.

I put a box on Bob's tripod, and we had a reading 'on TV.' They were SO scared. I asked a little boy to tell what he did last weekend - at the front of the crowded room. He began, "We were in the kitchen (Georgia accent) and a man came in the back door. I think he was my dad and he just got out of prison, and he took a butcher knife to my mom." I stopped him and said he didn't have to make up things to tell. He said, "I'm NOT." So I stopped that exercise.

I threw a piece of paper in the wastebasket - they dove for it because they had none at home and so it all started. I had students be the punctuation marks and act out sentences. I wouldn't let them go by the door of the principal. I came home *exhausted,* and Bob and the Art Department were there wanting to be entertained by my stories.

I gathered art supplies that were thrown away by the Art Department and everything else I could find to use. I couldn't deal with the Phy. Ed. equipment so I taught them to dance. On and on it went. THEN one day there was a knock at the door, and it was like a miracle. The principal presented a beautiful Little Girl in a gorgeous dress with her mother to join our class. Her mother was in hiding and getting a divorce and had purchased a house so Barbara would be at 'our school.' Things changed. She was most creative and very brilliant and became my soul mate and teacher's aide for all our ideas. I used to send three words home with her to write a story or poem. She has since written a play for Off Broadway. Refer to other stories of some of the things WE did. Years later she nominated me for a prestigious national award, and I WON. After the award, Siobhan and I went to New York for a wonderful get together, and she writes often.

Illinois to Winona, Minnesota and WSU Job

A few years ago - about 45 - I went to Minneapolis for an interview for a job at the U. I was going back and forth looking for an office number, and each time I had to pass a professor who was sitting outside. Each time I said, "pardon me," so he'd move his sprawled legs. Finally, I said, "Are you going to sit there all day?" He said, "I've been watching you - sit down and have a glass of tea." I did - and told him a tiny bit of my problems.

He said he knew of an opening perfect for me in a beautiful town named Winona. He thought it would be a perfect place for my 3 little girls and I to start over. I applied and got the job, sight unseen. I packed up my 3 girls in the VW convertible with the top down, and we set out for a new life. Can you imagine how many times I had to shift - from Texas to Illinois to Winona - all in our VW Bug Convertible?

I had managed somehow to pack everything for shipping, and we started out again for our 'new lives' in Winona. I had managed somehow to rent a house (over the phone from California). They had asked me which side of the tracks I wanted and where the girls were going to school?? It was like a foreign language - our next adventure.

Everything was to be shipped. When the furniture arrived the next day IT WASN'T OURS!! Ours had gone to someone in Wisconsin. We four slept on the floor, and the next two days the WSU Phys. Ed. Department came and straightened it out and helped unpack, and the bank showed up to loan us money.

Why I Love to Teach

Late on a Friday afternoon - the first week of Fall Quarter '95, I arrived at my office door after teaching two classes. One was Acting I, where I had announced that acting is 'lying convincingly' (a quote given me by a teacher a year ago - Alan Sneider). My students each told two stories - a lie and the truth, and we voted and discussed. This class was followed by an oral interpretation class. Each person brought an item and told how it was like them - their interpretation of themselves. It was very moving. They also gave a name to people they didn't know and described the voice that would come out of their mouth when first heard.

On my door were two notes. One saying, "Come to the costume room when you can; I think I found the skirt you want to use in Cinderella," the other was a note from a wonderful stage manager saying, "I've posted the list of casts on Call Board and marked all conflicts on the audition sheet."

In my office - all talking - all wonderful - were four students. Shawn L. came to show me his latest portfolio for his modeling agency and to tell his experiences this summer auditioning for movies. Shawn W. to tell me of his new graphics business he is opening in Winona and of his mother's newly self-designed home, including a beautiful desk with square nails created from a torn-down barn. Rachael, looking for a scene I did with her in Acting II, which she wants to use in Directing Class. Amy wanting to know whether I can get the driver again with the flat-bed for the Homecoming float and if she could write to get permission to turn Shel Silverstein poems into a musical.

The phone rang. It was Bart, a brilliant ex-student doing FAR advanced video in D.C. of the new plane to be used by the Pentagon (without pilot). His video was on TV lately. He's coming back, hoping to see Cinderella and to share his work.

This is why I love to teach.

Wheee, I've Almost Done It - Another Year!!

Sio is Great in the re-written Ibsen at Lanesboro. A real Bitch you'd hate. The play is excellent. Amazing blocking, set and lights. Michael, a student here years ago who now freelances all over doing lights - big success story. We both remembered how he nearly ruined thirty velvet hand-painted costumes designed by Cynthia, by pulling a string on a box of water that came pouring down. The theme was 'water' this year.

Alice was the best I've done. It was an odd script - 7 stages to go through to the Coronation. Sio said it was the first time she understood the book. 10 performances. I added touches for fun and a young audience - Comedian style - opened with 3 improvising clowns - a fun scene making the pepper soup that ended with a Sneezing Rap!!! And the Stage Manager turned on house lights and yelled, "Get on with the show!"

I found a genius guy who did all the sounds LIVE. Sat in costume and a special light on the side of the stage. I brought the tea scene up on the lift that wowed the kids. While it went down and got cleared, I had a great international storytelling act, and a few other things.

The costumes were Fantastic! Over half the cast were freshmen or transfers. Oh, I said I wanted a toy pig that could walk and grunt when the Duchess' baby turns into a pig. You can imagine the production meeting - Had a Fit. Santha found me the pig. It was a showstopper.

Speech Class Stories

I taught speech in the Old Library at WSU – a beginning class. I got the idea, "You have 5 minutes to go to find something that inspires a short speech." They all left – and returned. I called on a student that always has a twinkle in his eye. He began speaking and then raised his hand holding a gun and SHOT IT. We all fell to the floor, The LIBRARY CLEARED! He had gone to the Athletic office and borrowed a starter gun. I was removed from the library.

My class was held in a Frank Lloyd Wright Theatre-in-the-Round at Florida Southern. It was when I just met Craig (Don Vander-bilt). He sat in the front row of the circle. I could feel his eyes examining me, so I moved him to the back. I had assigned a persuasive speech. I knew he was not prepared, so I called on him first. He slowly got up and very slowly walked to the opposite side of the circle – paused – and laid down on one side resting on one elbow - to persuade us it was much more interesting and memorable to lie down to speak rather than stand behind a podium with half of your body covered. That was 58 years ago and thousands of speeches later, and I haven't forgotten.

Graduation from WSU Teaching

I'm considering trying to be a gardener - with 3 herbs, tomatoes, and rhubarb. I bought a fun little wire bike with baskets for the herbs, and maybe Shasta Daisies. Oh, and ordered a wooden wind machine "to be assembled." It may never get out of the box. I live on a path for the college kids from WSU to the bars, and every Thursday night the yard is designed with bottles, papers, bags, and pranks - like removing a big rock from the rock garden to the middle of the street, and bending a large iron sunflower over. George says if it happens again, we'll buy another and put poison ivy on it. It would be simpler to take up the piano again. Long ago, I would play the Maple Leaf Rag.

It stopped snowing in MN---maybe. I attempted to take some of my winter clothes to file in the basement and found so many ideas there waiting. I'll never live long enough to wear them all. I spend a couple hours a day at my favorite cafe, my social club. Eat the same thing, and people come by, and now I'm writing to you. It's a great escape. George's flight plans change daily but maybe I'll be going along to Florida for a week with the MATHY Jet.

Graduation is over – I made up all the grades, Sio and Peter are off with 25 students to Ireland. When they return, she goes into rehearsal – got caught in a play in Minneapolis. So, I get to "play" in Minneapolis with her for a week!!!

I have 1 semester and 1 play (Peter Pan with flying) to go before-

Love,
   Viv

P.S. It stopped snowing in MN - we think.

"Framed Nature" Art Show Opens

PUBLISHED IN WINONA POST, SEPTEMBER 2021

Vivian Fusillo opened her new show, "Framed Nature," at
the Acoustic Cafe in Winona.

Vivian Fusillo sees the world as art. She has been creating it in many forms her whole life. From starting a theatre while in college to her legendary career as a director at Winona State University, she also studied and designed costumes at Stratford-upon-Avon in England. She is known as well for her one-of-a-kind personal design creations which she accessorizes with her large rings, bracelets, and other jewelry pieces from all over the world that make her signature look. She is a life-long writer, watercolorist, and sometimes just goes ahead and creates her own medium, as she has done now. A taste of her newest works, "Framed Nature" are currently on display at the Acoustic Cafe and the Winona Arts Center. Fusillo has collected nature pieces as her palette and gives us yet another version of how to see the world through Vivian's eyes, where everything is art.

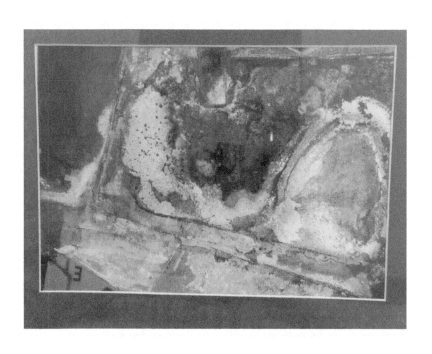

Vivian Fusillo's amazing legacy honored with theater dedication

October 7, 2015

From: Keith Polus, Scene shop foreman

Saturday evening the Performing Arts Center at Winona State University was filled with people whose lives have been touched by Vivian Fusillo, as the Performing Arts Center was being dedicated and named the Vivian Fusillo Theatre. It was an extraordinary evening. Four university chancellors were from past and present. Darrell Krueger, Robert Dufresne, Scott Olson, and the chancellor from the University of Eau Claire Wisconsin, James Schmidt. Gary Evans, the interim vice president for university advancement, was the master for the ceremony and was wonderful. Vivian has 46 years of theater directing at Winona State and many of her former students were there, along with many other individuals who have been touched by her performances. Her awards and accolades were numerous as she has touched thousands of children and adults alike. I personally have been in several of her children's shows from 1976-1987. There was a wonderful slide presentation that her children and grandchildren created spanning the 46 years, and we were even entertained with a performance from two of her grandchildren, Brooke and Bailey Bestul. Vivian always viewed young people not as empty bottles that needed to be filled, but as candles waiting to be lit. Thanks, Vivian, for lighting all of those thousands of candles. It was an evening that will always be remembered for those of us who were there, and if you were one of those unfortunate individuals who missed this weekend, her creations will now be with us for generations to come, having the Performing Arts Center now named the *Vivian Fusillo Mainstage Theatre.*

Part Seven

HEALTH

The Golden Shoulder

Oh, how my life has changed. I can't drive for 6 months, can't move my left shoulder for 6 weeks – not even in an expressive gesture. My skin is changing color and texture from all the pain pills I take every 2 hours day and night. A bowel movement is a neighborhood celebration!

From Mayo Doctors: "Do not move your left shoulder – you've had too much bone loss. We sculptured a large metal prosthesis and glued all the scattered bone pieces to it and tied the nerve ends – a most complicated operation." (In fact so complicated they used it for a demo at the national convention - I didn't sign a star release.) "I don't want to scare you, but if anything else happens, we can do nothing more!" Thank God for Mayo and insurance. My house cost $35,000, my shoulder $90,000. I guess I was practicing auditioning for the circus.

Before Christmas I had two days not seen by anyone. I drove to Lacrosse alone to see the matinee, Frieda – had no memory of it – I found a stub in my purse. Many tests showed nothing but perfect health.

Weeks later I awoke with unbearable pain in my left arm – Called George and he was in town, Thank God. We drove 110 miles an hour to Mayo. I had a seizure in the car, then another in the ER. I was in the hospital for 2½ weeks. The operation was 5 hours long.

I have never been in the house this much. Thank goodness for fairly clean windows and friends who bring gourmet food, and some rare experience with the home care help - like my first sponge bath by a handsome young man with spiked, bleached hair, jewelry and Over-White Teeth. He announced, "I'm from WSU. I've always wanted to be in the theatre." Ugh!

I go to sleep enclosed in many pillows, and my left side from neck to fingertips is covered with frozen packs of veggies – corn, peas, beans. I think the peas work the best. My new jewelry is 24 Big Silver Staples on a 10-inch slash on my shoulder. I'm anxious to get out and run and play.

Also, to hold the insurance, I'm not allowed to leave my house – except to get my hair done or church. I want to go to the movies – "NO." I told them to substitute because I don't go to church - "NO."

My First Liver Spot

I hadn't been in Winona very long and had started teaching at WSU. While living in England, I had a wig especially designed for me out of REAL hair by Raymond of London. I wore it to many evening events. It was styled so there was a curl touching my left eyelid in one spot.

Well, I noticed a brown spot on that eyelid, so I went to my first dermatologist for an exam. I met Dr. Bures, along with his many "toys" he used to amuse his clients. With my wig in my hand, I explained my concern that something in the wig had caused _the spot_.

He said, "Well, let's see." He put on the wig and continued on with his pranks. Suddenly he stopped, and pulling the wig off his head said, "Do you see anything yet?!"

313

365 Jewels Heart Shock

I, who am never ill, had a severe attack of stomach pains. I thought I had mad cow disease, so off to the sudden excitement of the emergency room. I had 90 miles an hour in a limo ride to Mayo. After six days of constant warm, friendly attention (I didn't even know how to work the bed), I was made ready for the electric shock to get my irregular heart in rhythm. I was rolled into the heart factory with 50 others to be given 100 jewels, 200 jewels, 300 jewels shock. No change.

That evening, a short military-type surgeon bet the other one $5 or two beers he could make it work by going sideways instead of straight (that's me). He came back in his best gray silk, Italian cut suit. I was the only patient on July 4th. He gave me 365 jewels and my <u>heart returned to normal!</u>

So now I'm Normal! Gotta stay in rhythm – no alcohol, chocolate, or coffee. (I had to hide my chocolate covered coffee beans.)

Gallbladder

Before this, I had NO idea where my gallbladder was or whether I had one. I was wheeled into the gallbladder recovery room (I could write a book on personalities of all the "wheelers" I've had), taken past six empty beds - all sectioned off by pale gray, paper curtains with tiny yellow flowers, that someone with bad taste had sold the entire hospital - with nurses chattering away while waiting for customers. I was wheeled to the far corner by a large window - shade pulled - into a very small space. I tried to listen to the nurse (I'm still without hearing aids and really feel off balance) telling me all that was to happen to me. I sort of heard...

1. Take Barium liquid.

2. Sit for ½ hour.

3. Something about a machine with a complicated name that I'd be put in for one hour while they filmed my gallbladder.

She smiled and quickly reached up and pulled down a TV, size

12x18, and pushed it 12 inches from my face (so I could hear I guess). I couldn't possibly look at Donald Trump that close. I looked surprised. She said, "Oh don't you watch TV?" So she turned the intruder off and opened the shade to a beautiful garden below. I only got a 15 minute view when a new wheeler man took me past seven watercolor paintings of trees. Note: I just returned from a 16-hour workshop on painting - landscapes. I HATE PICTURES OF TREES.

I ended up in a huge room with eight bed sections (same curtain dividers), all filled with sleeping recovery customers. A fun, wonderful nurse went from one bed to another shaking them gently awake. He used different words and voices on each. At a break, I asked him what he would say to me when I woke up. He patted me on the shoulder and said, "I'm not that lucky. I'll be off duty."

A huge, good looking black man, Mr. Black, came to my bed and said in a gorgeous base voice, "I'll be doing your gallbladder scan." I said, "I hope you find something." He looked very concerned and said, "I don't know." He'd probably been in on the meetings of GI doctors trying to decide whether I should have a gallbladder operation. He said, "I need your vitals." Name - he repeated it making it sound like I had never heard it said before. Age - he repeated the info. I said, "Shssh!" He threw his head back and laughed, showing his gorgeous set of white teeth. I was wheeled again past a new set of tree drawings. I was carefully tied down and placed with just my gallbladder section placed in the machine by two really fun nurses for 1 hour, while all the movement of my gallbladder was filmed.

I dozed off for a while and woke to the two nurses and a doctor watching the filming and making remarks about my gallbladder. I interrupted and asked if I could watch after I heard them say, "That's good," and later giggle. I had no idea there could be a joke about my gallbladder movement. I imagined them at their job, everyday watching people's gallbladders and whether they could recognize people by the film. They moved over and the four of us watching became a gallbladder party. It was in black and white and looked like fabric designs, but - No Jokes.

Rare Experiences in a Nursing Home for Two Weeks

A very handsome ex-student (they're everywhere) gave me a shower and also tended to all the details on the toilet, while he told me how much he liked my class.

I talked them into not one, but a second shower, but couldn't take Rose. She was 6' tall and weighed 260+. She sat to do my back and her stomach fell down!

Dr. Dufresne is there - sometimes with it but always clever. He wandered into my room and sat on the bed. I complained about the shower (down the hall). He said I could use his. We'd probably have to sign some papers, etc. I found out he didn't have a shower.

Was told to ring the bell for 'Help.' It took 35 minutes for help to arrive and NO idea what to do. My whole leg was SWOLLEN. Four were standing at the foot of my "too short for me" bed and said, "It's probably a blood clot. What do you want us to do?" I said, "Call a doctor?" "We aren't allowed to in the night."

I called George - on a flight in one of the jets. He said, "Do Nothing, I'll be there in an hour." The nurse had called an ambulance - $2000 - to take me to Mayo. The sirens roaring was entertainment for the whole house, those that could shuffle to the windows to see the excitement. George arrived, and with an offer of a couple beers, talked the ambulance guy out of taking me, etc, etc. I had 17 people not capable of waiting on me. I became so frustrated. I remembered I was a director and four were maybe capable of training. When I sat in the lounge chair it was broken so it didn't hold my legs up at all. What a mess. They couldn't or wouldn't take directions. The guy next door played awful music LOUD and burned popcorn every night. I went to a lower level (my level 4 was filled with many Overweight People) to get "knee therapy." They asked if I wanted to color while I waited. There was a man 'coloring.' He was half the size of an artist I once knew. He colored and said, "Abstract." He hadn't talked before. They were putting tape dressing on my whole leg trying to get the SWELLING down. Had I not been 'let out' the next day, I would have had him color my leg around the tape and we could have an art show.

When I was able to bend my knee enough to get my long legs into a car, I got to go for a ride OUTSIDE. What a Revelation!

I'm just beginning to get up out of a chair - or the toilet - using all my strength, which isn't much. I can't use my left arm and my right one has NO muscles, and my right, that knows it gets the next operation, hurts more than the New left knee, SO...

It's a mind thing. Using the handicap bars is useless in my case. I went to a Beethoven Concert and had to be lifted, Shari has sore ribs and George a sore back from that experience.

I was in a handicap toilet and no matter how much I thought I could push myself up, I was STUCK and had to call for help.

Lots of New Experiences

Another new adventure. I'm in Mayo getting a new knee.

The most beautiful human made is my doctor. He put his initials on my left knee (my first tattoo), so they'd get the correct one in the operation.

The 'after' pain was worse than having twins, except the end pain with no pretty twins.

Dr. DuFresne came by and wanted to kiss. He couldn't lean down, and I couldn't get up.

The Art of Aging — Through Dance

I don't remember what I tell whom, so if???? Just toss.

I went to a program called The Art of Aging, just to see how it was presented. I was "well dressed" in a warm sweater. I walked in and there were about 40 elderlies sitting in a semicircle, which included eight in wheelchairs.

An Old Time Band was playing, including an accordion player and a tiny woman playing a huge tuba. The leaders were a young girl - professional singer, a male dancer who looked 'ordinary,' not threatening, and an older Italian professional dancer. They were warming up the crowd by having them "dance" in their chairs. I stood in the background, and someone got me a chair, so I sat.

After warming up the audience, they encouraged some to get up and dance. One couple (who go to some dance every Saturday night) got up, and all but four got up and moved to the music. Oops, I forgot a Detail. When they asked us to get up, the male dancer rushed over to me and almost picked me up. I said I was recovering from a broken foot. He insisted that it didn't matter and pulled me on the dance floor for us to "lead" the others. I was so hot in that sweater and out of breath. He said, "I knew you were a professional dancer." Ugh! We did "several rounds" and I begged to sit. A woman, almost as wide as she was tall, came running over and said she always wanted to dance with a teacher. She said she went to WSU years ago - was not involved with theater but would come over between classes to see what I was wearing before I went to class. Amazing! Well, the most important part of this day is they offered me a job to tour with them. Maybe I have a future after all????

What's Next?

This is perhaps the most exciting part of my 93 years: I've had two strokes and a seizure. I always overdo things. The most exciting part is the loss of eyesight on the outside periphery of both eyes. I'll skip all the details. I am to do eye exercises for two months and may get more vision back. Meanwhile, everything I see is floating past back and forth, up and down. I'm sitting on the front porch (all sounds are magnified). The birds are knocking my ears off kilter and a boy just went by pulling a LOUD wagon. I almost lost it. A car image just drove through three houses and two trees across the street. Too bad I can't paint all these images! These letters may or may not stay on this page. I much prefer the 150 sounding birds to the Warland Singers, but I prefer lower notes.

At this point I can't read all the many cards and letters I have been receiving so George reads them to me. I wish he was an A in Oral Interp instead of a D - Oh well. All the ex-students going back 50 years are Keeping Me Alive with their wonderful cards and FB comments, giving me credit for what I'm sure I didn't do. Three beautiful, talented daughters, 60+ years teaching and wonderful connections with students that continue to support me. Now I sit on my front porch, listen to the birds ROCK and wonder - What's Next?

Quotes from Students Who Were Inspired by Vivian

Vivian inspired so many students/people over the years. They share their appreciation with cards year after year. Here is a sampling.

~

Dearest Vivian,

Vivian, you are part of the "village" that helps take care of me ... because every single postcard you have sent me is part of our refrigerator. My kids know you as "Mom's protector," who taught Mom THE SKY IS THE LIMIT and much, much more!! So thank you so much for always remembering me! Thank you for being part of the village that is raising my kids!

I love you, Vivian! Love, Heidi

Dear Vivian,

I wish we were back on stage: singing, yelling and laughing. Those were the good times. I send you my best wishes and a note to let you know I miss the GOOD TIMES.

Laurel Miller

Darling Vivian,

I never picture you anything but a Goddess – strong and sure. We all come to you as little baby seeds and you helped us grow into smart, strong, and sure adults. It's been one of the great joys of my life to know you – and to love you.

Hugs and Prayers,

Becky M.

Dear Indian Princess,

With the help of the Leaf Gods, we have made it through another year! And still looking forward to an even better and kinder one with more adventures - rule breaking and (probably illegal) surprises.

Are we getting older? Yes, we are! Are we getting better? Yes, we are!

Still your biggest fan!

Vince

Vivian,

Your sunshine has touched so many lives. Mine included. (Heart)

Regards,

Cheryl Pierre

Beautiful clothes and beautiful jewelry only realize their beauty on a beautiful woman.

— Jim B.

Dearest Vivian,

Now I realize I was unprepared for college and too immature to take advantage of the opportunities that were presented at WSU. Thankfully, I had you and your family...and YOU as a professor.

Love and respect always,

Serlealan Wise

Dear Beautiful Vivian!

Thinking of you and all your creativity makes me smile in the middle of some crazy times in our world. I am grateful for so many things you added to my world.

Carson Brooks

Dear Vivian,

Just a quick note to say "Hi!" and let you know that I always think of you and have such fond memories of WSU! The happiest times of my life were there!

Love and admiration ... always,

Serlealan Wise

Dear Vivian,

I think that I have saved every postcard that you have ever sent me. They deserve a place in the Smithsonian – as do you!!

Love, Kevin

Kevin Packer and Michael Hill

Dearest Viv,

Love and profound respect,

Blayn

Hello Vivian!

I hope you feel this "love rock" - Your love for life, creativity, exploration has rocked the world of so many and continues today.

Sending so much love,

Ginger and Stevie Kranz

Dearest Vivian,

We LOVE your postcards!

You look absolutely amazing, strong, and beautiful! My heart is filled with enormous joy when I see you and my kids - love to see your photos. We are all in agreement that you are SUPER COOL and I thank you for remembering me! I wish I could drop by your house and give you hugs and see your next creative project. I would tell you how much I've always admired you and feel so grateful to be one of your many students! I love you Dearest Vivian!

Love, Heidi (McCabe)

Dear Vivian,

    You are everyone's favorite!!

    I hope we can have playtime <u>soon</u>!

    Love, Catherine

Dearest Vivian,

    I was one of your students at Winona State from 1987-92. You taught me so much and shaped the way I've lived since college. Thank you for all you've done for so many theatre kids.

    Heather Edwards

Hello Viv!

    I am so happy I got to share some of the best years with you all. Of course, all the years have been the best!

    Smooch -

    Denny

Viv,

    You have given so much to those who had the pleasure to be in your presence.

    Dean Kephart

Dearest Vivian,

I'm sure you've heard from a number of former students and admirers, appreciators, and characters. (Smiley face) Vivian, you are so gloriously original, passionate, and fierce. I graduated in '89 and found you as not only a favorite teacher and director, but one of a handful of people who played a big part in shaping my life. Okay, your spaghetti dinners are pretty memorable too. One of the things I appreciated the most about you was your ability to enjoy people for who they were. You created a safe place for people to express themselves. That's truly a gift! My speech and theatre background has served me well over the years. I thank you for your part in making it possible for me to land my dream job! People actually pay me to talk! Who knew?!! Much love and many wishes for a smile or two a day as you work through this next chapter.

XOXOXO Sending hugs and well wishes from California!

Sarah Jane (Langness) Rohde

It is impossible to sum up, in a page or two, what I learned from Vivian. To say that what she taught affected my outlook on life in general, as much as it taught me about theatre specifically, sounds almost cliché, and yet it would be the truth. She taught me how to go after what I wanted and to reach for the stars, knowing that you can't get there at all if you don't even try. She taught me how to really look at the world around me and how to find my place within that world. She taught me how to see the world and how to use what I saw for the creation of art and, conversely, how my creation of art affected the world around me.

Daniel Munson

Hi, Viv,

Your postcard was so creative and charming, as usual. Know that I am sending love and gratitude for your imprint on my life. You spread such free flowing, creative spirit. Please take care of yourself and stay safe. We need you for inspiration.

Love, Debra Darby

Dearest Vivian,

You, my dear Vivian, stand next to me as I move forward in my teaching career. No other teacher has encouraged the belief in my voice as an artist as you did. In my early years as an actor, you encouraged bold choice and vivid embracing of the possibility in imagination. Thank you, thank you, thank you. Armed with a vivid imagination, so much is possible.

Love,
Blayn Lemke

Dearest Vivian,

Now is the time for me to inspire you! I know you are feeling the love all over the world being sent to you ... Drink it in. Your gifts and passion have inspired stories of living a creative life fearlessly from so many of your students. Your wisdom in unique clarity spoke to each of us personally. So, as you gain strength, know your legacy is spreading the joy of fearless creation around the world.

Love,
Blayn

I was a theatre major in the 1980s and I am still professionally engaged in speech and theatre. Vivian directed me in 10 shows and taught me in a number of classes. I learned three powerful, unspoken lessons that are crucial in the way she brought theater to life:

1. Creativity can be modeled, taught, and learned.
2. Excellence is hard work; so, work hard at it!
3. Practical details are important enough to give them attention.

I remember these lessons every day.
Phil Schmidt

Dear Vivian,

It's been an awfully long time! I want to thank you for being such an inspiration to me as a teacher, director, and human; and through the amazing experiences you gave me. I think of you often, the things you said and taught us. I often think, "What would Vivian do?"

Love,
Leslie (Dame), Class of 1984

Dear Princess Covered-With-Leaves,

I especially admire your reverence for the Winona Sioux tribal traditions – and Princess Winona. The old ways are the best!

Love,
Vince

Dearest Vivian,

I decided to audition for the Children's Production. When you walked in, Vivian, my heart leapt in my chest with joy. Here was this seemingly larger-than-life woman, dressed in a leopard print, with all kinds of jewelry that clinked and clacked when she moved. Then you put us all on stage and got us moving and getting to know one another through the breaking down of physical, mental and emotional barriers. My life had been saved. It's due in large part to the massive influence you have had on that university, and I am certain you have had only glimpses of the lives you have impacted. You gave me permission to be fully me, to be alive in who I am and who I was becoming. I couldn't be more grateful for you. I've lived a rich and full life. It doesn't all trace back to you, but it all passes through you and your loving, quirky, brilliant influence in my life.

I love you, Vivian. Forever.

Patrick Hoth

Very Dear Viv!

Rendezvous? Oh, how I wish!!!

So much love from your old Griffin Elementary pupil and forever fan,

Barb Crook

Dearest, Dearest Viv,

I deeply apologize for my grievous tardiness and am, as usual, impressed that you live up to the vivacity I and several others have always admired, sailing past "alleged" two strokes and a seizure, writing memorably your biography in bits and pieces, great force of nature that you are. I thoroughly enjoyed your dramatic "Top Secret TV Ad." Just another great addition to your legend.

(Heart, heart) Gary Luckert

Vivian,

Always remember, you helped to save my life, by helping bring me back to myself.

Much love and deepest respect,

Patrick Hoth

Vivian!

RULER OF ALL FABRIC ... GODDESS TITAN OF BOLD JEWELRY AND IDEAS ... INSPIRATION FOR MANY!

Sending love, love, love today and always. HEAL. Breath. Be patient.

I'll see you soon! Love you!

Kim Schultz

Vivian,

I miss you and your SPARKLE!

Kelly McGuire

Dear Viv, July 22, 2020

You have always been, and always will be in my humble opinion, a dynamo! Active, involved, and definitely your own unique and vibrant individual! I will always remember that day in college I was so stressed about something I couldn't control, and you saw how tense I was. You, in true Viv form, just walked up to me and started grabbing my hair at the roots and said something to the nature of, "You need to relax ... get some blood moving and don't take things so seriously." You pulled on my hair for a good bit as I recall; but it was probably only a few seconds – but those few seconds I have always carried with me. I remember that day every time I get too worked up about something that is beyond my control. Sometimes I even pull my own hair to try to get that blood moving. Thank you for that moment!

Love and Best Wishes,

Cheryl Pierre

Vivian,

You mentioned your clothes and jewelry. You have always been glamorous. Your bone structure is just gorgeous. A "fashionista" colleague of mine once said, "Living a fashionable life is so much more than the clothes you wear. It's also how you "wear" your values, experiences and morality." ... it is a different way to think of fashion.

Love,

Renee Neal

Dearest Vivian,

I hope your recovery is going well, because you're needed on stage for Act III. Don't miss your cue. I was thrilled to see your lovely face in the SquareSpace Commercial with Winona Ryder. Such a delight! Get well soon so you can do another one!

Much love from your Captain Lesgate!

Ole Ryan

Mrs. Fusillo, June 2020

Just a line to tell you that you had a real impact on this farm boy, and I use what I learned from you every day. I was lucky to have a few great teachers, with you and J.R. among them. Sure I remember the red hair, artful clothes and boas – but not so much as your senses of LIFE. I don't think you ever said it, but it came through - "Take those accidents of fate – ROLL with them!! Carpe diem is not adequate!!!" I taught it to our kids and now our grandkids. Thanks for all that.

Steve and Janet Peine

Dear Vivian, July 2020

My memory floats from cherished times when I had the honor of working with you on the first show we did at Winona State back in 1968, "Playboy of the Western World," where I was lucky enough to be called Director and you were brand new - and agreed somehow to be my costume designer, and Jacque Reidelberger formed the set out of practically nothing. Your creativity was always a marvel to me and something that meant so much to so many of us. A big regret is trying to understand my lost years without you. I love you Viv, and am so grateful to know you.

All my love,

Mario Lorenz

Dear Viv,

Remember, you are still you, and nothing short of amazing and glamorous and always will be. Remember how fabulous you are!!!

Love,

Debra Darby

Dearest Vivian,

As I've now gone on to share theatre with hundreds of young people every year, and all over the country, you can be certain that a little Vivian Fusillo flows in the blood of all those children. Many of them are adults now and parents themselves. Some are performing on Broadway and others are making movies and television shows. We don't always know how it's going to turn out, but theatre has taught us that the show must go on. You've lived that lesson and we're all better for it. Just know that you're a part of the thousands of children out there continuing to discover themselves through theatre in my classroom, as are all the children benefiting from so many theatre students who came before and after me in your classes and shows.

I never got a score lower than the one I received in your class the spring in '89. Funny how the one theatre class I ended up blowing off, Theatre of the Classroom, ended up being the thing I would do most in my career. And funny how our embrace that fall of '91 would be the thing I remember better than any of your classes or the shows we did. I wish I could get one more of those right now.

With love,

Chris Mahle, WSU 1987-94 (on and off)

Dear Vivian, August, 2020

I love you, Vivian. The music I have included made me think of you, and the title of the music composed on the CD is called Resilience.

All my love,

Mario

Dear Vivian,

I think of you often, Vivian. You have been a strong beacon of light in my life for 40 plus years. I've always admired your zest and curiosity of/for life and you are always an inspiration to me. And to that I say, Thank You.

My Best, Kevin

Dear Viv, Oct, 2020

How excited I was to see you in the Super Bowl ad for Winona! Obviously, you looked great and exactly how I remembered...do you actually age? Seriously, you looked fabulous! How fun that must've been for all who know you...I know I had pride for knowing you and spending time in Winona! Seriously, I was telling everyone I know to watch for the Winona commercial and look for my AWESOME theatre professor!

Much love and great memories of you always,

Cheryl Pierre

Hi Viv!!!

The best way to tell you the positive influence you've had in my life is to WRITE about it. So this is very much a "THANK YOU" for being in my life and continuing to be a significant influence.

I was immediately enchanted, encouraged, and enthused (it would cause me to become a double major!) watching the instructor interact with students already there whom she obviously knew from previous classes. That instructor was Vivian Fusillo and meeting her would have a quiet, subtle and deeply profound effect on the whole rest of my life.

Viv believed in the concept to "**use the whole building**" and **involved audiences** the minute they stepped into the venue or even onto the grounds with outside signage and even characters or props curbside. I had learned that message well ... It was lovely! She approved. I got an A which bolstered my confidence. Thanks, Viv! Viv insisted that part of my theatre minor must be ON stage. At Viv's request, I created a **"lobby show"** for *Quilters*. I dressed in period costume and handed out a small piece of fabric to EVERY audience member. I understood the value of involving your audience. Thanks, Viv, for that opportunity. Always do something a little different, make it pertinent, and make it memorable. Thanks, Viv! Thanks, Viv!! You're still the best and still our Golden Lady!

Julie Zuehlke, WSU 1983 Grad

Hi Viv!

As the 2019-20 school year comes to an end, I've reflected on the people who shaped my life. You have been a force of nature! You have inspired me and generations of students/colleagues to embrace beauty, life, and creativity.

Love,

Julie

Hey Viv, March 21, 2020

I purposely didn't send you one of the store bought "Get Well" cards. As I looked at them I could hear you saying, "These are just dreadful. Who would be cheered up by such depressing cards?" I laughed out loud in the card section and then found this more beautiful card instead – it reminds me of you and all of your beauty!

Much love,

Brian Hodge-Rice

Dear Vivian!

I tell students about you as my favorite teacher!
Thinking of you. With love,
Kerri Westhauser

Dear Viv,

You have touched the lives of so many children and brought them joy! The glowing ball of joy you have created will continue to expand infinitely. More than this, you have inspired, nurtured, and believed in the creative and joyful child in me, and I know, in all your students. I have been so grateful for your influence, support, and mentorship throughout my life, in good and difficult times. The example you offer, your love of life, beauty and the creative spirit is infectious. Viv, I hope to keep in touch with you more, and I can't wait to be inspired again by your "Second Act." Curtain up, it's your new opening night.

With much love and gratitude forever,
Debra

Viv,

(Postcard of Zion National Park)

These colors made me think of you. Natural, glowing, texture patterns ... Beautiful!!

Kelly McGuire

Greetings!

Congrats on the "spot" on the Winona Ryder "extended" video – LOVED IT! Especially seeing you in it; sent it to family and friends -

Until next time, your student,

Serle Wise

Viv!

How was your anniversary? Did you make a special dress? Dance under the stars? Most likely shined just as bright as those stars!

All my love,

Shawn

Dear Vivian, May, 2005

I just wanted you to know that there is no need to thank me for the article I wrote. The pleasure was all mine. When you have someone so inspiring to write about, it is nearly impossible to suffer from writer's block, so I cannot take all the credit for a job well done. Although I have just met you, it is obvious that you are an amazing woman who has led a very interesting life. Bearing witness to the positive influence you have had on so many lives was inspiring, to say the least. You are a woman with much wisdom to share, and I was very honored that you took the time to share some with me. I had a wonderful time visiting with you and learning about your life. Your home was very warm and inviting, especially on such a cold, rainy day.

You shared with me that day that you are always looking for new friends, so hopefully there is still room for one more!

Take care and keep in touch,

Andrea Northam

Viv could touch a piece of fabric, and as we discussed a costume for a cast member, I would be inspired to create what she wanted to see on stage! Just like she inspired her students to act and be successful in life! Thank you my queen!

Carl Stange

I wasn't a good actor, but I remember Vivian seizing on my ability to replicate whatever I heard, verbatim. I don't think she called me a parrot, but she had some great quip about it. I do recall her calling me the third twin.

Ginger Kranz

At home, when things start going crazy, we always say, "Pull a Vivian and PAUSE.... PAUSE..... PAUSE... now go!"

Zendyn Duellman

Vivian had a very strong influence on me in college. She was always able to inspire me in so many creative ways as an actor, a director, and a writer. Now that I'm a teacher myself, I think of her often as I work to inspire others artistically.

Forrest Musselman

"That's either the best thing I've ever seen or the worst thing I've ever seen. I can't decide." I have a feeling she said that often. When asked if she thought I should pluck/wax my unibrow to create two separate eyebrows she said, "Put a bandaid between your eyes for a few days to try it out. She led me to believe I was an actor. She so convinced me that I have been a professional actor for 36 years. I begin understudy rehearsals at the Guthrie Theater for The Tempest in a few weeks. She appears to have been right.

Love to you, Viv!

Jon Hegge

She became my favorite instructor, mentor, coach, role model, and friend right then -- and she didn't even know it yet either. We eventually became colleagues as well. I graduated in 1983 and returned to WSU in 1985, hired onto the staff as Director of News Services and eventually onto the faculty in Mass Communication two years later. I have always kept my connection with the Theatre Dept. and Vivian.

Julie Z.

"Mem to Viv" I'll call it!

A very key person in my life whom I still greatly admire. I declare you my "G-MOAT" (Greatest Mentor Of All Time)!

Forever grateful,

Julie Zuehlke (WSU 1983)

There's SO much more, so many more stories and so much more to say "Thanks, Viv!" about – and I know when to bring the curtain down! Leave 'em wanting more. So until next time: THANKS, Viv!! You're still the best and still our Golden Lady!

Julie Z.

Hello Vivian,

I hope this finds you well. You may not remember me, but I was thinking about Aunt Sponge and what fun it was; especially since Meryl Streep is now doing it for charity. Thank you for making my time at WSU so special. I was chatting with Kelly, Lisa, and Chuck Michel today. We hope to reunite there soon.

Love, Jon Schaefbauer

I'm sure many students in the performing arts have gained and learned from you – but I am one who gained from you in the performance of life.

Lisa, 1983

I want to thank you so very much for touching my life in such a very special way. Through your smiles, enthusiasm for the unique, unexpected and refreshing and extraordinary talent for blending all of the beautiful gifts you have for bringing out the very best in people in a production of Cinderella.

Robbin Brent

As Vivian's Assistant Director for Wizard of Oz, I felt I observed a true 'pro' at work! Her ability to command – not demand – the cooperation and respect of cast and crew alike was really quite amazing to me. Many of the students had told me not to miss taking a class from her as she was an excellent instructor.

Lois Roberton, 1979

Thank you for sharing the Beauty of your being!

With Love, Tim

Vivian,

Everything you have fostered through all these wonderful years - the love, energy, frustrations, laughs, moments of brilliance, hours of thought, with and without sparkles, have forged that theatre into greatness. You have directed more than plays, you have directed hearts and minds - moved souls - and cemented friendships.

Shawn

Congratulations! You have changed the lives of thousands—and so, again have we – through your teaching and allowing....

Love Fran, '09

You are different Vivian, and before I met you I had no idea how to channel my creativity and zany ideas, and you gave me the strength to not be ashamed of the way my mind works. You make me feel like I can do anything and I am able to do that because of you.

Monica, 2005

Keep shinin' and flying—and inspiring the rest of us to jump a little bit higher. I am so proud to have had you as my teacher, and toward the very start of your amazing journey.

Barb Crook

Thank you again for another splendid evening of entertainment. I marvel at your talent to cast students, and your very professional talent of developing character in a play. On behalf of WSU, thank you, Vivian. You are one of the best.

Jack Kane

If you have been lucky enough to have had Viv as an influence in your life then you know what it means to suddenly experience the world in entirely new and mind blowing ways - like a power boost to the 5 senses that lasts the rest of your life.

Rachael Cavegn & Keith Kryzer

After a long rehearsal night Vivian gets to me for notes and says, "You did something amazing, and then you screwed it up!" Successes and failures exist so close together they almost overlap. The greatest teachers let you experience both.

Jared Wills, Class of 2004

Dear Professor,

Today I planted two daylilies. I am calling them the Professor Vivian Lilies, named after a woman I love a great deal and who has been my role model for my entire adult life.

Denny Bell

Vivian is an inspiration to all of Winona. Her reputation exceeds the boundaries of the school. She makes you want to be in theatre and when you're in her class you feel supported and know you can take a risk without being made a fool. This is the mark of a good teacher. Having students who go on to work is also a mark of a good teacher. I have been lucky enough to work at such great theatres as The Guthrie, McCarter Theatre, Arena Stage, The Old Globe, Theatre de la Jeune Lune, The Jungle, The Ordway, guest star roles on NBC's ED and LAW AND ORDER and in film HERMAN USA and most recently shot IN SEARCH OF MYSTERY and ABSOLUTE TRUST. She did a great job for me. Thank you Vivian!

Rosalie Tenseth

Vivian teaches that creativity is everyone's birthright..., and that living can itself be a highly theatrical act, and that theatre is but one great way to perform a life. I echo the sentiments of many of Vivian's past and present students that she was the single most important, motivating force in shaping their lives.

John Blondell

Vivian's generous nature, vast life experiences, and wonderfully quirky sense of adventure have been an inspiration to me for the past fifteen years, and she continues to be an important part of my life today. It is without hesitation that I recommend her for this prestigious award. I only hope that these few words can express even a hint of how much Vivian's friendship has meant to me.

Randy O'Neill

2002 ACTF competition - I was luckily selected to compete for the Irene Ryan Acting Scholarship, and the night of Prelims the announcements were made around 8 pm and my name got called - jumping for joy I looked around, didn't see Viv. She had gone back to her hotel room to take a bath, so she comes out of the hotel room with a white bath towel wrapped around her head and rushes downstairs as my "advisor" to find out next steps for semifinals. She looked amazing as if she planned her outfit that way. This woman always made every situation fun, and devoted her time to students!

Jared Wills

I'm grateful for you,
Kim

Vivian was much more than a teacher in my mind. I can not recall a day in my life that I have not used lessons, words or ideas instilled to me by her. She has shaped and inspired my journey to not only a better life but to be a better person along the way. For this I am forever grateful.
Brad Schwichtenberg

I hope you know that you continue to be a bright star for me in the Winona Sky.
John

The angels in your life are not from central casting, Vivian. They are the spirits of those you have touched in a most meaningful capacity.
Jim Brust

Awards Vivian Received

- Kennedy Center/Stephen Sondheim Inspirational Teacher Award, 2015
- Lifetime Achievement Award for Arts, Communication and Theatre Association of Minnesota, 2009
- Creative Drama Award, The American Alliance for Theatre in Education, 2006
- Oscar Brockett Outstanding Teacher Award in Higher Education, Association of Theatre in Higher Education, 2005
- Outstanding Women of the Arts and Humanities, Winona Fine Arts Award, 2001
- State of Minnesota Public Service Award for Distinguished Service (WSU Children's Theatre), given by Rudy Perpich, 1988

Plays Directed by Vivian Fusillo

(WINONA STATE UNIVERSITY)

1968-1969 Ali Baba and the Forty Thieves

Ali Baba and the Forty Thieves 1968-1969

1968 A Moment, A Mood
1969-1970 Theatre of the Mind
1969-1970 The Wizard of Oz

Wizard of Oz 1969-1970

1970-1971 Theatre of the Mind - Sensitivity

1971-1972 Theatre of the Mind - Time

1970-1971 5 Minutes to Morning

Five Minutes to Morning 1970-1971

The Hobbit 1971-1972

1971-1972 The Hobbit

1971 Sight and Sound
(Multimedia Workshop)

1972-1973 Theatre of the Mind - Playground

Theatre of the Mind, Playground 1972-1973

1972-1973 Alice in Wonderland

Alice in Wonderland 1972-1973

1973-1974 Trudi and the Minstrel

1974-1975 Tango

1973-1974 Theatre of the Mind - Magic

1974-1975 Children's Theatre of the Mind
1974-1975 Theatre of the Mind -
Voices in the Attic

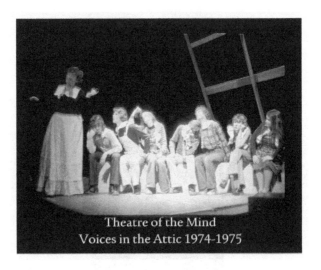

1974-1975 Peter Pan

Peter Pan 1974-1975

1975-1976 Othello

Othello 1975-1976

1975-1976 Theatre of the Mind - Dreams

1975-1976 Nicolo and Nicollette

1976-1977 Arsenic and Old Lace

Arsenic and Old Lace 1976-1977

1976-1977 Theatre of the Mind -
Paper, Processing and Packaging

Theatre of the Mind
Paper, Processing and Packaging 1976-1977

1976-1977 Ten Tales

Ten Tales 1976-1977

1977-1978 Scapino

Scapino 1977-1978

1977-1978 Theatre of the Mind - Words

Theatre of the Mind
Words 1977-1978

1977-1978 Wizard of Oz

1978 wsu children's theater
presents

the
Wizard
of Oz

may 10-12 7:30 pm
performing arts center
reservations required
information 457-2121

The Wizard of Oz 1977-1978

1978 Ten Little Indians

1978-1979 The Good Doctor

The Good Doctor 1978-1979

1978-1979 Theatre of the Mind - Eyes

Theatre of the Mind
Eyes 1978-1979

1978-1979 The Thwarting of Baron Bolligrew

The Twarting of Baron Bolligrew 1978-1979

1979-1980 Richard III

Richard the III 1979-1980

1979-1980 Theatre of the Mind - Toto, I've a Feeling We're Not in Kansas

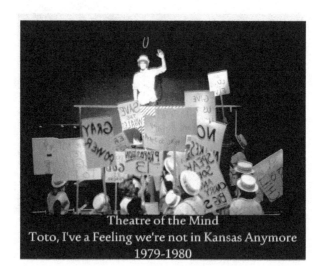

1979-1980 Our Own Backyard

1980 My Three Angels

Equus 1980-1981

1980-1981 Equus

1980-1981 One Life to Live

Theatre of the Mind
One Live to Live 1980-1981.

1980-1981 Oliver Twist

1981 Front Page

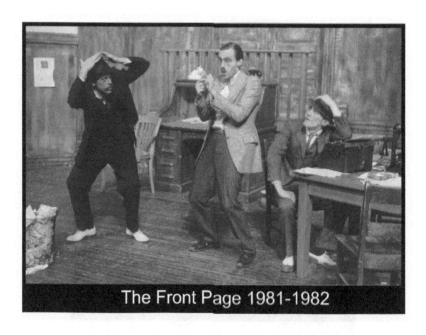

1981 On Golden Pond

On Golden Pond 1981

1981-1982 Theatre of the Mind - Heroes

Theatre of the Mind Heroes 1981-1982

1981-1982 The Lion, the Witch, and the Wardrobe

The Lion, the Witch, and the Wardrobe 1981-1982

1982-1983 Of Mice and Men

Of Mice and Men 1982-1983

1982 Mark Twain Remembers

Mark Twain Remembers 1982

1982-1983 Cinderella

Cinderella 1982-1983

1983-1984 Our Hearts Were Young and Gay

Our Hearts Were Young & Gay
1983-1984

1983-1984 Theatre of the Mind - Emotional Forms

Theatre of the Mind
Emotional Forms 1983-1984

1983-1984 Peter Pan

Peter Pan 1983-1984

1983 The Man Who Came to Dinner

The Man Who Came to Dinner 1983

1983 Rusty in the Square
(Walker Art Center)

1984-1985 The Brick and The Rose

The Brick and the Rose 1984-1985

1984-1985 Roots to Wings

Roots to Wings 1984-1985

1984-1985 Theatre of the Mind - Hats

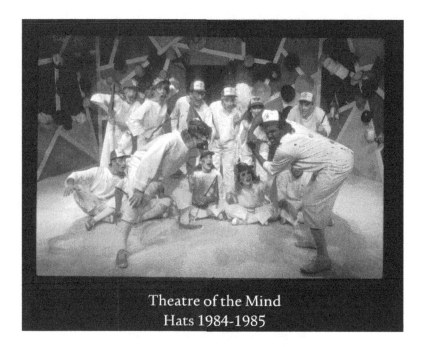

Theatre of the Mind
Hats 1984-1985

1985 Nicolo and Nicollette

Niccolo and Nicolette 1984-1985

1985-1986 A Christmas Carol

A Christmas Carol 1985-1986

1985-1986 The Dark Castle

The Dark Castle 1985-1986

1985-1986 Theatre of the Mind - Water

Theatre of the Mind Water 1985-1986

1986-1987 Rainmaker

The Rainmaker 1986-1987

1986-1987 Theatre of the Mind - Choices and Changes

Theatre of the Mind Choices and Changes 1986-1987

1986-1987 Rumpelstiltskin

Rumpelstiltskin

May 6-8, 1987, 7:30 p.m.
Winona State University, Performing Arts Center
For Reservations Call (507) 457-5235

Rumpelstiltskin
1986-1987

1987-1988 Quilters

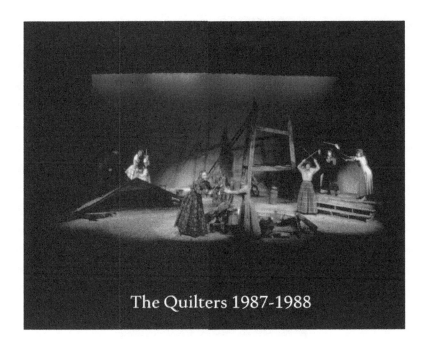

The Quilters 1987-1988

1987-1988 Theatre of the Mind - Food

Theatre of the Mind Food 1987-1988

1987-1988 James and the Giant Peach

James and the Giant Peach 1987-1988

1988-1989 Eleemosynary

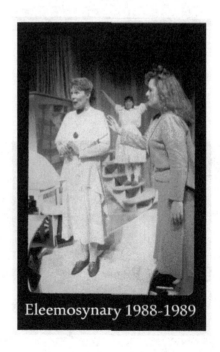

Eleemosynary 1988-1989

1988-1989 Tall Tales

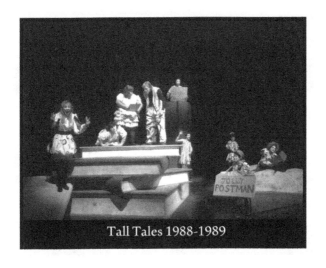

Tall Tales 1988-1989

1988-1989 Theatre of the Mind - Attitude

1989-1990 Treasure Island

The Adventure of Treasure Island 1989

1989-1990 Theatre of the Mind - Animals

1990-1991 Christmas Carol

A Christmas Carol 1990-1991

1990-1991 Theatre of the Mind - Windows and Walls

Theatre of the Mind
Windows and Walls 1990- 1991

1992-1993 Ali Baba and the Forty Thieves

Ali Baba and the Forty Thieves 1992-1993

1992-1993 Dial M for Murder

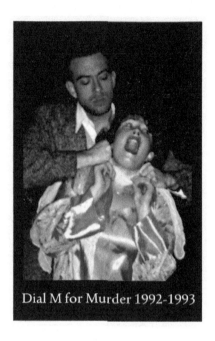

Dial M for Murder 1992-1993

1993-1994 DanceScape 93-94

DanceScape Ritual Voices (with Gretchen)
1993-1994

1993-1994 Around the World in

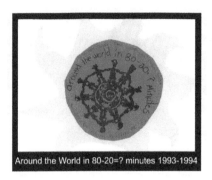

Around the World in 80-20=? minutes 1993-1994

60 Minutes

1994-1995 Pinocchio

Pinoccio 1994-1995

387

1995-1996 Cinderella

Cinderella 1995-1996

1995-1996 Hamlet

Hamlet 1995-1996

1996-1997 Many Moons

Many Moons 1997

1997-1998 Timeless Tales

Timeless Tales 1997-1998

1997-1998 Phenomenal Women

Phenominal Women 1997-1998

1998-1999 Thirteen Clocks

Thirteen Clocks 1998-1999

1998-1999 Identity Crisis (Capstone)

Identity Crisis 1998-1999

1999-2000 Macbeth

Macbeth 1999-2000

1999-2000 Rumpelstiltskin

Rumpelstiltskin 1999-2000

2000-2001 A Christmas Carol

A Christmas Carol 2000

2000-2001 The Importance of Being Earnest

The Importance of Being Earnest 2000-2001

2001-2002 The Good Doctor

The Good Doctor 2001-2002

2001-2002 The Dark Castle

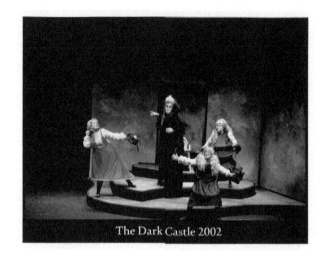

The Dark Castle 2002

2003-2004 Thieves' Carnival

Thieves Carnival 2003

2003-2004 5 Minutes to Morning

2004 Wizard of Oz

2004-2005 The Taming of the Shrew

Taming of the Shrew 2004-2005

2004-2005 Trudi and the Minstrel

Trudi and the Minstrel 2005

2005-2006 Mousetrap

2005-2006 Many Moons

Many Moons 2006

2006-2007 The Effect of Gamma Rays on Man-in-the-Moon Marigolds

The Effect of Gamma Rays on Man-in-the-Moon Marigold
2006-2007

2006-2007 James and the Giant Peach

James and the Giant Peach 2007

2007-2008 Tales Told Round the World

Tales Told Round the World 2007-2008

2007-2008 Medea

Medea 2007-2008

2007-2008 Thirteen Clocks

The Thirteen Clocks
2008-2009

2008-2009 Imaginary Invalid

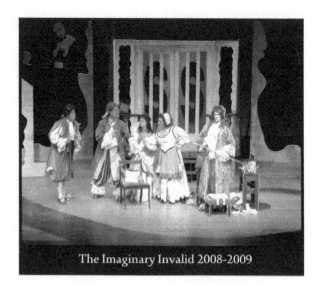

The Imaginary Invalid 2008-2009

2008-2009 Alice in Wonderland

Alice in Wonderland 2009-2010

2009-2010 Ali Baba and the Forty Thieves

Ali Baba and the Forty Thieves   2010-2011

2011-2012 Treasure Island

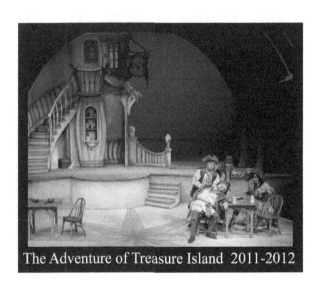

The Adventure of Treasure Island 2011-2012

2012-2013 Rumpelstiltskin

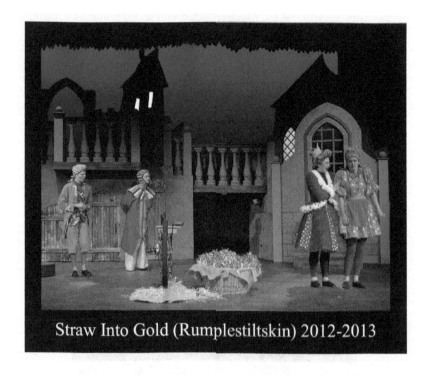

Straw Into Gold (Rumplestiltskin) 2012-2013

2013 Peter Pan

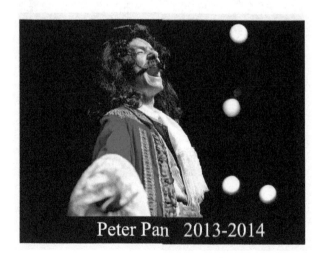

Peter Pan   2013-2014

Made in the USA
Monee, IL
04 January 2023

24547996R00227